Gramsci's Marxism

Pluto **Press**

Carl Boggs

Gramsci's Marxism

First published 1976 by Pluto Press Limited
Unit 10 Spencer Court, 7 Chalcot Road, London NW1 8LH
Copyright © Pluto Press 1976
ISBN 0 904383 03 2
Printed by The Camelot Press Limited, Southampton
Designed by Richard Hollis, GrR

Contents

Preface / 7
Introduction / 11

1. **Marxism as the 'Philosophy of Praxis'** / 21

2. **Ideological Hegemony and Class Struggle** / 36

3. **Mass Consciousness and Revolution** / 55

4. **The Factory Councils: Nucleus of the 'New State'** / 85

5. **The Revolutionary Party: 'Modern Prince' and 'Collective Intellectual'** / 101

Epilogue: Gramsci's Marxism Today / 119
References / 127
Index / 143

Preface

Antonio Gramsci's theoretical work has received greater and greater attention in both Western Europe and the United States over the past several years, owing mainly to its conceptual advances within Marxism and its strategic relevance to movements for liberation in the developed capitalist societies. Though Gramsci's writings were scarcely available to non-Italian readers before the 1960s, his ideas already have had a remarkable impact in a number of countries. They have shaped the thinking of Marxists like André Gorz, Lucio Magri and the *Il Manifesto* group in Italy, Lucio Colletti, Louis Althusser, Ralph Miliband, and Eugene Genovese, and have become part of the intellectual and political debates in journals such as *New Left Review*, *Il Manifesto*, *Socialist Revolution*, *Radical America*, and *Liberation*. Almost totally unknown less than a decade ago, Gramsci is now being taught in many university courses and seminars in political and social theory around the country, particularly since the appearance in 1972 of an extensive English translation of the *Prison Notebooks*. A three-day conference on Gramsci's Marxism was held at Washington University in St.Louis in February 1973, attracting a wide range of panellists and more than a hundred scholars, activists, and other interested people from the Midwest and East. The conference, which one journalistic report misleadingly referred to as the birth of 'Gramscism', provided the springboard for a semester-long seminar on various aspects of Gramsci's thought in the sociology department at Washington University, attended by twenty-five faculty members, graduate students, and undergraduates.

What became readily apparent at the conference and, even more noticeably, during the many weeks of the seminar, was the absence of anything remotely approximating a shared understanding of what Gramsci was about – his philosophy, his central theoretical motivations and guiding concepts, his relationship to other Marxists, the political relevance of his work, and so on. There was a uniformly high degree of enthusiasm for exploring Gramsci's theory, and it is probably safe to say that most of the conference and seminar participants were attracted to it out of previous political commitment. But the priorities, interpretations, and prescriptions for political action differed so vastly that many began to wonder whether there was in fact any real unifying thread to the theory, any compelling reason to study Gramsci in the first place. Some people came out of the seminar confused and frustrated, feeling that somehow they weren't able to grasp the true meaning of Gramsci's Marxism; others fastened on to one or another *segment* of his thought, seeking to apply it to specialized interests; still others viewed Gramsci as primarily an *Italian* theorist whose contributions were meaningful only within a particular historical-geographical context. The diffuse and fragmentary nature of Gramsci's writings no doubt helped to create this situation, as did the intellectual and political differences of the participants themselves. Yet there was still another factor: very little interpretative secondary work in English had been done that could situate Gramsci within the Marxist tradition for those far removed from the Italian and Western European scene of the 1915–1935 period. Unlike Lenin or Mao, Kautsky or Lukacs, Gramsci still remained mysteriously *foreign* – despite the immense breadth and theoretical sophistication of his work. This has been true despite the excellent historical and biographical treatments of Gramsci produced by John Cammett (*Antonio Gramsci and the Origins of Italian Communism*) and Giuseppe Fiori (*Antonio Gramsci: Life of a Revolutionary*).

The present volume is an attempt to help fill that gap. It seeks to illuminate Gramsci's thought by isolating and exploring crucial themes, drawing broad comparisons with other dominant tendencies within Marxism, and establishing some rather explicit linkages between theoretical premises and political strategy. What is the genesis and meaning of concepts like 'ideological hegemony', 'organic intellectuals', 'myth prince', and 'revolutionary historical bloc'? What is the problematic of mass consciousness that Gramsci raises, and how does it inform his approach to the factory councils and the revolutionary party? In confronting these issues, I have found that a definite thematic continuity underlies Gramsci's theoretical work from the early period to the *Prison Notebooks* – a continuity that far outweighs the change in priorities and emphases that mark different historical 'stages' in his political life. What it amounts to is a remarkably powerful advance towards a comprehensive Marxist theory of cultural revolution, one that is among the most valuable we have. To evaluate Gramsci in this way means looking at the broad contours of his theory rather than the fine points that are deeply enmeshed in historical and biographical detail. This is an interpretative exploration, not a systematic exposition.

The main impetus for this book grew out of a two-part article I wrote on Gramsci's *Prison Notebooks* for *Socialist Revolution* (nos. 11 and 12, 1972) and an earlier article on Gramsci's thought and the American New Left that appeared in *Liberation* (January 1971). Some of the original framework remains, but revisions and additions (for Chapters 1, 2, 3, and 5) are extensive; the Introduction and Chapter 4 (on the councils) are completely new.

Since my interest in Gramsci has evolved out of more than a decade of political involvement and theoretical search, it is very difficult to pinpoint the many influences (intellectual stimulation, events and activities, personal relationships) that have inspired the writing of this volume. Certain recent influences do stand out, however. The Gramsci conference and seminar furnished many fresh ideas and approaches and helped me to bring together what in my own mind were some previously vague or disconnected aspects of Gramsci's thought and Marxism in general. My colleagues at Washington University who shared this experience and who have been helpful in general include Pedro Cavalcanti, Paul Piccone, Richard Ratcliff, and David Sallach; a number of visitors also contributed, particularly Alastair Davidson, Juliet Mitchell, Geoffrey Nowell-Smith, and Leonardo Salamini. Two other teaching colleagues at Washington University, John Kautsky and Mark Selden, have helped me in countless ways through their intellectual presence, friendship, and encouragement. In many cases, my relationships with students have been the most rewarding of all; I have found that teaching and learning have been equal and dialectical parts of the same process. In this respect, I am particularly thankful to John Ainlay, Kevin Dougherty, Lew Friedland, Harold Karabell, Gail Pellett, Judy Raker, Tom Shapiro, and Patricia Tummons — all of whom participated in the Gramsci seminar. I also wish to express my gratitude to the *Socialist Revolution* collective — especially Paul Joseph, John Judis, Karl Klare, James Weinstein, and Eli Zaretsky — for much enlightening criticism and comradely support. Roderick Aya has been a constant source of encouragement and editorial assistance. Lillian Ehrlich has done an outstanding job of typing the manuscript, often under the most trying and pressing conditions.

Others I would like to thank are Joseph Herring, who was my research assistant, Devereaux Kennedy, Terry Koch, and Raymond Pratt. My greatest debt of all is to Gail Pellett, who inspired my work and taught me how to see things a little more clearly.

Carl Boggs
St. Louis, Missouri

Introduction

It is one of the strange paradoxes of Marxism that a theory which has shaped and inspired the greatest revolutionary movements of this century has at the same time given birth – particularly in the most advanced capitalist societies – to a remarkably powerful non-political and even anti-political tradition. Many if not all of the major historical splits within Marxism have in one sense or another revolved precisely around this basic issue: whether politics should be conceptualized as the reflection of 'deeper' economic and social processes in a society, or whether it has (or should have) an independent and creative role to play in socialist transformation. Both approaches can find ample justification in the writings of Marx and Engels, particularly in view of some of the theoretical ambiguities that have arisen in part out of the unfinished nature of their work, in part out of their failure to confront systematically the problem of political power. What might be called 'anti-political' Marxism took different forms among the early Marxists – the economism and gradualist reformism of Bernstein, the 'scientific' materialism of Plekhanov, Kautsky, and the Austro-Marxists, and the spontaneism of Rosa Luxemburg. One or another of these tendencies dominated the Second International and the more recent variants of Social Democracy, the later phases of the Comintern and the Communist parties of contemporary Western Europe and elsewhere, post-revolutionary Marxism in the Soviet Union and Eastern Europe, and even the syndicalist and anarchistic alternatives that have challenged these established, deradicalized Marxist movements in a number of countries. Everywhere such tendencies have met with one failure after another. And to the extent that Marxism has made its presence felt in the United States, its character has generally assumed anti-political dimensions, often combining economist, spontaneist, and mechanistic theories in the most bizarre ways.

It was of course Lenin, through both his conception of a highly-organized vanguard party and his imaginative leadership that guided the Bolshevik conquest of power in Russia, who initially asserted the 'primacy of politics' within the Marxist tradition. By seeking to resolve, in the context of political struggle, the basic inadequacies and dilemmas of classical Marxism, Lenin opened up new avenues for exploring revolutionary strategy; he politicized Marxism by rescuing politics from its long theoretical and practical submergence as a mere by-product of the economic 'base' and raising it to the level of a positive historical force, a creative mechanism of socialist revolution.

But most of the old anti-political biases in Marxism still hold sway, and it is astonishing how meagre have been the efforts to develop a politically-strategic Marxism. Hostility to politics has been so great that even those theorists who have deviated most from orthodox Marxism and who chose to explore new intellectual paths, such as Korsch, Lukacs, Marcuse and the other representatives of the Frankfurt School, and Marxist 'humanists' like Sartre and Kolakowski, themselves ultimately rejected the political realm (and thus any systematic concern for revolutionary strategy) out of their preoccupation with the philosophical and cultural aspects of the superstructure. The surprising fact is that only one major Marxist writer has penetrated this theoretical impasse to broaden, 'democratize', and enrich Lenin's strategy of socialist revolution – the Italian Communist Antonio Gramsci, who died in 1937 after spending the last ten years of his life in Mussolini's prisons. It was Gramsci's persistent refusal to deny the political component of the revolutionary totality, either as the result of qualitatively new historical circumstances or under the impact of his profound interest in philosophy and culture, that constitutes his unique importance to the Marxist tradition.

Gramsci's immense theoretical output can be traced through four rather distinct stages. The initial one, which covers the period 1916 to 1919, encompassed the formative years of Gramsci's political and intellectual maturation: his involvement in the Turin working-class movement, his active membership in the Italian Socialist Party

(PSI), his exposure to Crocean idealism, his first attempts to grapple with the causes of the failure of traditional Marxism. This was also a crucial period in the early development of the Italian left, since it included the participation of Italy in the war, the socio-economic breakdown and crisis of authority that followed the war, the unprecedented revolutionary ferment, and the subsequent decline of the PSI as severe factionalism and indecisiveness led to paralysis at the very moment of new political opportunities. However, Gramsci's prolific writings during these years (most of which appeared in *Avanti!* and *Il Grido del Popolo*) touched upon a wide range of topics that went beyond immediate political events – most notably philosophy, culture, and Italian history – but their journalistic format inevitably worked against any elaborate theorization.

The second period spans the dramatic months of the *Ordine Nuovo* (New Order) movement in 1919–1920, when mass strikes, factory occupations, and the rapid spread of the council movement in Turin opened up what Gramsci saw as a 'new era in the history of humanity'. Gramsci and a small nucleus of Piedmont Marxist intellectuals (the *Ordinovisti*) started the journal *L'Ordine Nuovo* in May 1919 for the explicit purpose of giving theoretical expression and political direction to the militant spontaneous struggles of Turin workers after the war. Gramsci at this time was probably more intimately involved in the everyday life of workers than at any other time in his political experience, and his *Ordine Nuovo* writings reflect this. Despite the failure of this insurgency to push beyond the provincial boundaries of Turin, and its eventual isolation from the rest of the Italian left, the *Ordinovisti* provided a rich theoretical legacy which has given inspiration to European working-class movements. The contributions Gramsci made at this time, which raised his intellectual work to a new level of sophistication, were many: his brilliant critique of the PSI and the Marxism of the Second International, his analysis of the role of political parties and trade unions in the development of capitalism, his articulation of the theme of councils (*consigli di fabbrica*) and soviets as new forms of socialist democracy, his elaboration of the concept of 'dual power' and 'prefigurative struggle' in the revolutionary process, and so on.

The years of 1921 to 1926, from the founding of the Italian Communist Party (PCI) to Gramsci's arrest and imprisonment by the fascist regime, mark the third stage of Gramsci's political-intellectual development. With the entrance of most of the *Ordine Nuovo* group into the PCI, Gramsci now moved into national politics in Italy and quickly emerged as one of the dominant intellectual forces within the PCI leadership. During this period a good deal of Gramsci's energies was consumed by the ongoing and bitter factional struggles in the party around the question of political strategy, which was usually bound up with the rivalry between Gramsci and Amadeo Bordiga. In addition, Gramsci, who spent much of the 1922–1923 period in Moscow, became deeply embroiled in the tense conflict between the Comintern and the PCI. From 1923 on, Gramsci's attention (and that of the entire Italian left) became increasingly focused on the menacing rise of fascism and the very survival of the PCI itself. During much of this time Gramsci was able to continue as editor of *L'Ordine Nuovo*; but many of his writings also appeared in the PCI daily *L'Unità* and in the party's theoretical journal *Stato Operaio* (*Workers' State*). Understandably, they centred around the concrete exigencies of party strategy and tactics in a political context of urgent demands and rapid change.

And finally, there is the period of prison confinement, isolation, and physical torment that spans the years 1926 to 1937, representing the culmination of Gramsci's theoretical work at the very time of his greatest depression and sense of impotence. Gramsci began writing his 'notes' (the *Quaderni del Carcere*, or *Prison Notebooks*) in the prison at Turin, in February 1929 and continued his labour on them intermittently until 1935 when his deteriorating health made sustained concentration impossible. In all there were 32 notebooks consisting of 2,848 pages (4,000 when typewritten), which covered a vast range of topics – Italian history, education, culture, philosophy, the role of intellectuals, theory of the state, the position of women, Catholicism, etc. But the central and guiding theme of the *Notebooks*, which combined fragmentary notes and observations with systematic analysis, was the development of a new Marxist theory applicable to the conditions of advanced capitalism.[1] Though unfinished and unpolished, they still bear all the marks of Gramsci's brilliant and penetrating mind; and their significance for Gramsci's own life can hardly be emphasized enough. As Fiori states in his biography of Gramsci:

> For Gramsci, this work became life itself: these memoranda and brief notes, these sketches of the first germ of ideas, these tentative ideas left open for endless development and elaboration, were all his way of continuing the revolutionary struggle, his way of remaining related to the world and active in the society of men.[2]

As we shall see, these four phases in the evolution of Gramsci's life and thought represent quite different sets of priorities, theoretical emphases, and responses to the political world, that vary not only with changing events and issues but with the gradual maturing of Gramsci's ideas over time. The gap between his pre-prison and prison writings is particularly great. Until late 1926, virtually all of Gramsci's intellectual work was closely tied to everyday political struggles – first in the PSI, then in the *Ordine Nuovo* group, and finally in the PCI; for this reason the writings of the first three stages were directed more concretely to issues, personalities, and conflicts of the moment, and often assumed more of a journalistic character. The *Quaderni del Carcere*, on the other hand, were written from a perspective of detachment, isolation, and distance from the factional debates within the PCI and the Comintern; because of this and the obvious pressures of censorship, the writings of this period were for the most part more theoretical, more sweeping in their historical scope, and sometimes more vague. No longer preoccupied with immediate events while in prison, Gramsci, despite the many hardships he faced, was now able to step back and draw theoretical lessons from his years of political experience. If there is in the *Quaderni* little of the sense of urgency that characterized much of Gramsci's earlier writings, they do have an openness and depth that is usually lacking in his pre-prison work.

Yet it is essential to stress that, despite these historical variations, there is an overall theoretical continuity to Gramsci's Marxism through all four stages. What the *Prison Notebooks* most often reflect is a theoretical elaboration of concepts, insights, and historical observations contained in the earlier works. The image of 'two Gramscis' (or even 'three Gramscis') that some commentators have fashioned is valid only at the most superficial level of changing issues and priorities; philosophically, there is nothing even remotely resembling a sharp discontinuity or 'epistemological break' in Gramsci. (It must also be remembered that Gramsci's intellectual output, unlike that of Marx or Lenin, spanned only twenty years.)

The important point here is that several dominant themes consistently reappear in Gramsci's thought, from the initial exploratory articles in *Avanti!* to the imposing philosophical formulations in the *Prison Notebooks* – themes which, taken together, constitute the corpus of Gramsci's unique contribution to Marxist theory and strategy. They are the following:

1. Gramsci was above all a *creative* Marxist who never failed to seize upon the active, political, or 'voluntarist' side of theory in contrast to the fatalistic reliance upon objective forces and scientific 'laws' of capitalist development that had been central to the Marxist tradition. Gramsci was convinced, after witnessing the failure of the Second International, that socialist revolution would not come mechanically from the breakdown of the capitalist economy but would have to be *built*, that is won through purposive human action within a wide range of historical settings. The transition to socialism could not be expected to follow any unilinear pattern. And like Korsch, Gramsci argued that such a realization necessitated a new (reconstituted) philosophical foundation for Marxism which would restore the subjective dimension to socialist politics and place human actors at the centre of the revolutionary process.

2. As a Marxist who valued the transformative potential of politics, Gramsci always wrote as a *theorist of revolution* – which is to say that he transcended the realm of historical analysis and empirical description, strictly speaking, and insisted upon raising issues of strategy and political methods necessary to *destroy* bourgeois society. All of Gramsci's major historical studies were explicitly keyed on a single problem: the movement toward socialism. To put it another way, Gramsci's theoretical work was *dynamic*, embracing a dialectics of change and a strategic content that is again perhaps only paralleled in Lenin before him.

3. One of the most persistent themes in Gramsci, which becomes visible even after the most superficial acquaintance with his writings, is the fundamental Marxist concept of *praxis*. For Gramsci, this uniting of theory and practice, thought and action, subject and object was not only a guiding theoretical premise but was also central to his own personal-political life. Revolution therefore demanded not only rational-cognitive activity, but a passionate, emotional commitment and an intense partisanship on the part of the theorist – a commitment and partisanship rooted in everyday political struggle. This spirit of engagement permeated Gramsci's entire intellectual life, as a passage from one of his prison letters to his sister-in-law Tatiana Schucht clearly revealed:

> My entire intellectual formation was of a polemical nature, so that it is impossible for me to think 'disinterestedly' or to study for the sake of studying. Only rarely do I lose myself in a particular strain of thought and analyze something for its own inherent interest. Usually I have to engage in a dialogue, be dialectical, to arrive at some intellectual stimulation. I once told you how I hate tossing stones into the dark. I need an interlocutor, a concrete adversary, even in a family situation.[3]

4. Throughout Gramsci's writings, the role of *ideological struggle* in the revolutionary process looms very large – an emphasis reflected in the concept of 'ideological hegemony', the dominant and probably the most original construct in his work. In Gramsci's view, class domination is exercised as much through popular 'consensus' achieved in civil society as through physical coercion (or threat of it) by the state apparatus, especially in advanced capitalist societies where education, the media, law, mass culture, etc. take on a new role. To the extent, therefore, that 'superstructural' phenomena such as beliefs, values, cultural traditions and myths function on a mass level to perpetuate the existing order, it follows that the struggle for liberation must stress the task of creating a 'counter-hegemonic' worldview, or what Gramsci called a new 'integrated culture'. Gramsci insisted that socialist revolution should be conceived of as an organic *process*, not an event (or series of events), and that *consciousness transformation* is an inseparable part of structural change, indeed, that it is impossible to conceptualize them as distinct phenomena. (The problematic that Gramsci sets up here anticipates themes that have become integral to the development of Critical Theory and the rise of the Frankfurt School, and qualifies him perhaps as the earliest revolutionary theorist of advanced capitalism.)

5. Gramsci stressed that revolutionary change can be authentic only insofar as it is *total*, embracing all aspects of society, all dimensions of human existence. Most previous Marxists, though not Marx himself, had focused on a single aspect — usually the economic — whereas Gramsci introduced the notion '*ensemble* of relations' that incorporated economics but also included politics, culture, social relations, ideology, etc. For Gramsci, absolutely no realm of bourgeois society was outside the class struggle, no set of human concerns (no matter how 'mythological' or 'superstitious') was irrelevant to socialist politics; each dimension, moreover, was closely interwoven with all the others, so that the struggle to change one is inevitably bound up with the struggle to change all, i.e. the totality. (Gramsci's theoretical originality here, though never systematically developed, once again anticipates some of the later tendencies within Critical Theory, notably in Marcuse.)

6. One of Gramsci's overriding objectives was to articulate a vision of revolutionary transformation that was popular and organic, since he sought to overcome the elitist and authoritarian deformations inherent in the 'Jacobin' model (i.e. what is now defined as classical Leninism). This meant the development of a *mass* party rooted in everyday social reality and linked to a broader network of popular structures (e.g. the factory councils and soviets) instead of a highly-centralized vanguard party built exclusively for the purpose of seizing state power. Thus, in the Italian situation, Gramsci argued against Bordiga's ultra-Leninist conception of a tightly-organized elite party and emphasized a self-conscious process of popular revolt within the working class and peasantry that would prefigure the new communist society by creating the nucleus of anti-capitalist social relations, culture, work and authority structures *before* overturning the bourgeois state. This notion of transforming everyday life as part of the immediate tasks of revolution has its parallels in the theory of the early Wilhelm Reich and the 'Council Communists' (Pannekoek, Gorter) of the 1920s.

7. Another of Gramsci's consistent aims was the creation of a specifically *Italian* Marxism that would constitute the indigenous expression of a powerful 'national-popular' movement. Gramsci suggested that for revolution to become a truly popular phenomenon it would have to assume a *national* character; theory, in other words, would have to take into account the unique aspects of Italian history and culture, would have to offer a unifying perspective, and would have to develop a language that spoke to the customs, needs, and aspirations of the Italian people. Though he was committed to internationalism as a basis of political solidarity and long-range struggle, Gramsci rejected the mechanical borrowing of strategic models from abroad and even more the attempt (for example, by Stalin) to impose worldwide models from a single centre. And though he was strongly influenced and inspired by the Bolshevik Revolution, and by Lenin, Gramsci always cited the vast differences between Russia and Italy, between pre-industrial and European capitalist settings. Gramsci's preoccupation with diverse themes in Italian history and culture (e.g. the Risorgimento, the 'Southern question'), in linguistics, and in the writings of Machiavelli stems mainly from this sensitivity.

8. One of the most conspicuous features of Gramsci's Marxism, both in its style and content, was its 'open' and *non-sectarian* quality – rare then as today. His goal was to build a theory that would be visibly relevant to the broad masses, that would not arbitrarily exclude all ideas, innovations, and discoveries of bourgeois origin, and that would not contemptuously reject the spontaneous or 'primitive' stirrings of protest and revolt among the popular strata. What distinguished Gramsci's theoretical work from most of his contemporaries was its searching, probing, tentative character; attempts to construct a closed system consisting of scientific certainties, absolute truths, and formal abstractions could only isolate Marxists from the masses and stultify the creative processes of revolution. For these (and other) reasons Gramsci opposed 'abstentionism' (non-participation of socialists in bourgeois institutions) as a form of infantile leftist dogmatism.

This is the overall thrust of Gramsci's political thought – the broad outlines of a Marxist theory of cultural revolution for the advanced capitalist societies – which will be further explored in the following chapters. The themes summarized here constitute a new theoretical-strategic paradigm in the history of Marxism, despite Gramsci's own failure (no doubt the result of his prison confinement and early death) to articulate them as such. It is the paradigm of a revolutionary model that is simultaneously political and structural, cultural and popular. Theoretically, it represents an advanced critique of the economist-reformist and positivist-fatalist tendencies of orthodox Marxism; at the same time it incorporates but transcends the twin extremes of spontaneism and Jacobinism in forging the synthesis for a mass ('national-popular') revolutionary movement; and in its emphasis upon combining philosophy and politics, ideology and structures, analysis and strategy it avoids the one-sided and partial focus within much of the Critical Theory tradition. At the same time, it must be conceded that Gramsci's intellectual work, though voluminous, was never systematically developed and that his writing style, which at its best was rich and even poetic, was more often abstruse and fragmentary. Many readers of Gramsci have found his writings extremely difficult to bring together into any coherent theoretical whole. A good part of the trouble can be attributed to literary form (e.g. journalistic essays, pamphlets, prison 'notes'), but much of it also inheres in Gramsci's 'open' conception of the theoretical enterprise itself. Gramsci himself would have been the last to suggest that he had succeeded in working out a body of revolutionary theory that contained all the answers. What does emerge from a repeated and empathetic reading of Gramsci, however, is a very broad theoretical synthesis that suggests a particular orientation towards the crucial questions of socialist revolution in contemporary bourgeois society. It is a theory that inspires new ways of thinking about revolutionary politics and specifies a whole set of priorities – but a theory that nonetheless has to be extended, 'filled in', revised and developed to meet the imperatives of new conditions.

1. Marxism as the 'Philosophy of Praxis'

As soon as the young Gramsci launched into serious theoretical work during his early socialist period in Turin, one of the first intellectual tasks he took up was that of helping to restore the philosophical unity of Marxism that had been undermined by the 'scientific' orthodoxy of the Second International. This preoccupation Gramsci never abandoned throughout his lifetime, even if at times it receded into the background because of more demanding political responsibilities. The *Prison Notebooks*, which represent the culmination of Gramsci's intellectual work, are devoted largely to the goal of reconstituting the 'philosophy of praxis' on firm philosophical foundations. Like three of his contemporaries – Lenin, Korsch, and Lukacs – Gramsci reacted against the prevailing tendency to seize only the materialist, economic side of Marxism in a never-ending search for natural, uniform laws of historical development; he struggled to restore the elements of praxis and totality to Marxist theory by reintegrating the active or 'subjective' dimension without which the revolutionary process itself could not develop.

Gramsci's Marxism was nurtured in the idealist setting that had dominated Italian intellectual life before the First World War. There was of course the omnipresent genius of Benedetto Croce, whose philosophical thinking and historical analysis had a strong impact on the theoretical development of most Marxists (as well as non-Marxists) of Gramsci's generation. Perhaps even more important was the work of Antonio Labriola, who alone in Italy around the turn of the century sought to rediscover the unity of theory and practice that had been the core principle of Marx's own philosophy. While at the University of Turin, Gramsci became attached to the Hegelian perspective shared by Croce and Labriola and thus was increasingly critical of the objectivist theory expressed by the leaders of his own

Italian Socialist Party. For Gramsci, the break with positivism and all of the scientific pretensions of orthodox Marxism came early and left a permanent imprint on his thought. In repressing both the 'political' and 'philosophical' components of Marxism, the vulgar materialist conception of the transition from capitalism to socialism could in Gramsci's view lead only to political quietism and passivity. Gramsci saw in the popularity of mechanistic Marxism in Western Europe before the war a response to the sagging spirit of social democratic parties a source of certainty at a time of political retreat; thus, 'I have been defeated for the moment, but the tide of history is working for me in the long run.' Or, as Gramsci added: 'When you don't have the initiative in the struggle and the struggle itself comes eventually to be identified with a series of defeats, mechanical determinism becomes a tremendous force of moral resistance, of cohesion, and of patient and obstinate perseverance.'[1]

What the cult of scientific analysis had done to Marxism was to dull the critical edge of theory by rendering it abstract, divorced from action consequences, devoid of any strategic thrust. Gramsci concluded that, because of the undialectical relationship it posited between subject and object, thought and action, this deformation was as much the enemy of revolutionary Marxism as was philosophical idealism, which had opposed the unity of theory and practice from the opposite direction. In fact, however, it was mechanistic Marxism that had achieved such enthusiastic acceptance after the turn of the century, partly because Marxists needed a firm intellectual basis from which to counter the various religious and metaphysical ideologies that were integral to the popular world-view. What often emerged from the early philosophical struggles through which Marxism was seeking its ascendancy in the intellectual universe was the most simplistic materialism – an epistemology that reduced the sphere of ideas and consciousness to epiphenomena, mere reflections of objective historical forces. Following Labriola, Gramsci argued that the extreme terms of the debate around the dichotomy idealism vs. materialism, voluntarism vs. determinism, subject vs. object, etc. were shallow and misleading, and that any viable revolutionary theory would have to fuse (or actually transcend) both polarities.

The common tendency of isolating one fundamental component of human existence and making it supreme — either the philosophical ('idealist') or economic ('materialist') side — only served to transform theory into what Gramsci called an 'empty metaphysics'. On the idealist side there was Croce, whom Gramsci criticized for employing a 'pure conceptual dialectic' devoid of any concrete historical content; on the materialist side there was Bukharin, whose sterile 'laws of causality' and search for an eternally valid system of empirical regularities, led him, in Gramsci's characterization, towards an anti-historical form of 'flat evolutionism'. In this context Gramsci sought to restore the meaning of the dialectic as a unifying force in a new revolutionary Marxism, as a corrective to both speculative idealism and narrow empiricism, either of which could only capture history from the perspective of detached, inert categories. Gramsci pointed out that when Marx took over the dialectic from Hegel, he did not *replace* the idealist with the materialist dialectic as is commonly supposed, but in actuality integrated the materialist dimension into Hegel's dialectic, a very different process. Neither a strictly idealist dialectic nor an empiricist social science could comprehend historical movement as the struggle of opposite forces: both therefore involved a 'radical denial of politics'.

Gramsci's philosophical work thus sought to revitalize Marxism by returning to the spirit of Marx himself and opposing him to the one-dimensional theoretical current that developed after his death. At no time in his intellectual development did Marx ever counterpose science to philosophy, material conditions to consciousness; it was precisely his conception of revolutionary praxis that transcended the classical dichotomy between materialism and idealism. In his critique of Feuerbach and the French Materialists, Marx had attacked the dualism of mind and matter, mental activity and external reality — a dualism that undermined the possibility of conscious human intervention in history and led to a kind of political withdrawal. If the social world is not the product of creative human activity, how then can any kind of revolutionary change take place? The strict reflectionist view of knowledge and consciousness that later found its way into the theories of Engels, Plenkhanov, Kautsky, and the Austro-Marxists was antithetical to Marx's own dialectic. Nor did Marx ever systematically advance a model of socio-political development based upon a set of scientific laws; in fact, his analysis of the passage from feudalism to capitalism was very loosely-outlined, and he never really got around to specifying the nature of the transition from capitalism to socialism. There were certainly no determinate 'laws' or stages of development in Marx, much less a 'dialectics of nature'.

The degeneration of Marxism into different manifestations of scientism and economic determinism coincided with two related factors: the decline of revolutionary prospects in Western Europe by the turn of the century and the integration of the major socialist movements (most notably the German Social Democratic Party) in the most developed capitalist societies. Theoretical attention was no longer focused on the dynamics of the revolutionary process itself but rather on the internal functioning of capitalism as such. As the actual historical situation of the proletariat failed to validate the more optimistic expectations of nineteenth century Marxism, many socialists sought a kind of fatalistic deliverance in the quest for 'scientific truth'; science itself became a kind of faith in the leading sections of the Second International. Theory became an academic project, remote from and even hostile to political practice – part of a materialist paradigm that excluded all 'subjectivity', including philosophy, psychology, culture, the role of consciousness, and even creative leadership. Immobilized by this fetishism of science, the parties of the Second International failed to take advantage of the wave of revolutionary opportunities that swept Europe after the First World War. Only the Bolsheviks in Russia, who had long since overturned what Lenin had called 'legal' or 'textbook' Marxism, were able to achieve success in this moment of crisis.

Gramsci had sensed the paralysis of the PSI in Italy even before the débâcle of 1919–1920, when the party's strong reformist wing had blocked political initiative that might have effectively mobilized the vast majority of workers against the bourgeois state. Already during the period 1916–1917 Gramsci began to emphasize the crucial importance of consciousness in laying the foundations of socialist revolution; just as the Enlightenment paved the way for the French

Revolution, so too could a vast Marxist 'intellectual-moral' renewal lead toward socialism. Thus in his 'Sotta la Mole' column for *Avanti!* Gramsci devoted particular attention to the issues of culture and education; it was here that he first articulated his influential Marxist critiques of Pirandello and the futurists. And Gramsci's first widely-read piece of work, *La Città Futura*, set forth a lengthy criticism of the 'scientific superstitions' of positivism and argued for the role of will, action, and vision over mechanistic attempts at prediction. *Revolutionary* theory involved above all looking ahead into the future, which meant that facts, social conditions, and events could not be understood as something 'external'; they would have to be ordered by a set of moral principles, values, and political direction in such a way as to produce a specific historical meaning. He regarded orthodox Marxism as a psuedo-science, a 'form of arid mysticism' that sought to conceal the actual political weaknesses of the proletariat and in the end created an indifference around a false sense of security that history was favouring the revolution. *La Città Futura*, a pamphlet written only months before the Bolshevik Revolution, stands as Gramsci's earliest full statement in opposition to the simplistic materialism that had permeated Marxism.[2]

The Bolshevik conquest of power in Russia had an explosive impact on the Italian left during the period 1918–1920, and Gramsci was among those who heralded this as a world-historical event of monumental proportions. Aside from its obvious political significance, Gramsci interpreted it as a profound theoretical rupture with the past as well, which he analysed in one of his most important *Avanti!* articles in late 1918.[3] The Russian upheaval, in Gramsci's opinion, constituted in many significant respects a revolution *against* Marx's *Capital*, which had become an abstract, mechanistic treatise lacking any active political content. Until 1917, Marx's classic analysis of capitalist development had been more a textbook for the bourgeoisie in Russia than a theoretical-strategic guide for any revolutionary movement; among other things, *Capital* had presumably explained why Russia would have to experience the long, gradual evolution from feudalism to capitalism before socialism could be placed on the agenda. It was a fatalistic perspective that all but the most anti-positivist Marxists had come to accept. But in one historic episode the Bolshevik Revolution dramatically repudiated the entire body of elaborate, self-confident predictions based upon the 'laws of *Capital*', overturning with it the mythical powers of economic determinism. For Gramsci, Lenin and the Bolsheviks could be defined as *living* rather than *abstract* Marxists who seized historical initiative through self-conscious action, who acted upon the actuality of the Revolution instead of waiting for material conditions to 'ripen'. Political action had outstripped the lifeless, positivist Marxism that was supposed to serve as a framework for revolutionary praxis.

Gramsci's notion of the 'Revolution against *Capital*' was stressed repeatedly in subsequent articles that appeared in *Avanti!* and in *L'Ordine Nuovo*; it also inspired his later philosophical work in the *Prison Notebooks*, where he developed much further his critique of orthodox Marxism and outlined his general premises for a 'philosophy of praxis'. In the *Notebooks*, Gramsci attacked more systematically than ever the notion that a theory of revolution could rest upon materialist foundations, opposing to it the conception of an *active* political knowledge incorporating an awareness of human needs, objectives, and consciousness expressed historically through the dynamic of creative subjectivity. He criticized the attempt within Marxism to arrive at regularized, standard, or uniform patterns of behaviour, contrasting to it a praxis rooted in the dialectic and human will.

The main thrust of Gramsci's philosophical critique in the *Notebooks* was directed against those who, like Plekhanov and Bukharin, sought to create of Marxism a science that explained historical change by reference to a formal system of causal laws. These theorists had assumed a set of principles governing historical development that was external to subjective perception and action – an external objectivity of the 'thing in itself'. For Gramsci, however: 'Reality does not exist on its own, in and for itself, but only in an historical relationship with the men who modify it, etc.' Such epistemology merely became a substitute for concrete analysis of class and political forces in *specific* contexts; as reified theory, it could never lead to an explanation of actual historical events because it did not take account of the subjective side of praxis. Beyond that, it tends to destroy the revolutionary impulse itself by making the theoretical enterprise into a detached form of activity. Gramsci's argument was that the theorist whose role is shaped by the scientific ethic, or by the search for sociological laws and mathematical formulas, begins to develop an instrumental approach to knowledge and sooner or later loses touch with the realm of mass politics:

> Indeed in politics the assumption of the law of statistics as an essential law operating of necessity is not only a scientific error, but becomes a practical error in action. What is more it favours mental laziness and superficiality in political programmes. It should be observed that political action tends precisely to rouse the masses from passivity... So how can it be considered a law of sociology?[4]

Gramsci further suggested that positivistic Marxism of this sort would exercise an even greater depoliticizing influence under conditions of advanced capitalism, since

> With the extension of mass parties and their organic coalescence with the intimate (economic-productive) life of the masses themselves, the process whereby popular feeling is standardized ceases to be mechanical and causal (that is produced by the condition of environmental factors and the like) and becomes conscious and critical.[5]

In developing his conception of knowledge throughout the *Prison Notebooks*, Gramsci always incorporated the political, conscious active dimensions; he observed that people are not moved on the basis of theories derived from statistical laws – even if such laws could be formulated – but according to their 'active and conscious co-participation', their experience of 'immediate particulars' (feelings, sentiments, everyday needs) that tends to resist and break through abstract categories. A major problem in the search for highly-regularized patterns of behaviour, Gramsci noted, was the necessary assumption that the 'great masses of the population remain passive (so they can be studied by the scientists'), which of course cannot be squared with revolutionary praxis.[6] A better approach would be to identify certain broad 'tendencies' operating in a given society, a knowledge of which might facilitate political intervention in a particular direction and lay the basis for strategy and tactics. But even these objective conditions would only become historically operative once they were comprehended as part of a totalizing revolutionary process, at the moment they were taken into the minds of human beings, given shape, and applied to immediate political situations.

One politically destructive consequence of this scientific attitude, as Gramsci understood it, was that it tended to divorce theory from history by raising techniques and methods of analysis to an independent status, as ends in themselves. Theoretical abstraction could be defended on general philosophical principle, but never as a truly *revolutionary* enterprise. If the prevailing structures are to be transformed as well as analysed, they must be comprehended in time and space, seen as part of discrete (and variable) historical processes rather than as part of some kind of abstract universal order. Taking a position similar to that of Korsch,[7] Gramsci questions how in fact it was possible to distinguish between the theoretical and practical-historical components of Marx's own work. Did not Marx himself write in the *Theses on Feuerbach*, that:

> The question whether objective truth can be attributed to human thinking is not a theoretical but a practical question. In practice man must prove the truth, that is, the reality and power, the this-sidedness of his thinking. The dispute over the reality or non-reality of thinking isolated from practice is a purely scholastic question.[8]

Because Marxism embodies a conception of praxis, the 'laws of tendency', as Gramsci put it, have simultaneously an historical and methodological character. 'It is not enough to know the *ensemble* of relations as they exist at any given time as a given system,' he argued. 'They must be known genetically, in the movement of their formation. For each individual is the synthesis not only of existing relations, but of the history of these relations.'[9] Marxists who seek to establish universally valid systems of thought, who spend their time building neat, logically consistent formal models, ultimately mystify rather than illuminate history by ignoring the unique configurations that emerge through the variations in socio-political development. They also overlook the crucial fact that intellectual processes themselves – of whatever kind – are part of a complex and unique history that is shaped by particular cultural and political traditions, and that such traditions exert a powerful influence upon the scientific pursuit itself insofar as they embody a human consciousness that reduces Marxism to its historical dimensions. Thus:

> It has been forgotten that in the case of a very common expression [historical materialism] one should put the accent on the first term – 'historical' – and not on the second, which is of metaphysical origin. The philosophy of praxis is absolute 'historicism', the absolute secularization and earthiness of thought, an absolute humanism of history. It is along this line that one must trace the thread of the new conception of the world.[10]

From the perspective of transcending the religious or 'metaphysical' survivals of traditional philosophy, Gramsci viewed the strict materialism of scientific Marxism as no more of an advance than the 'idealism' of Hegelian Marxism. One central premise of the former was the existence of a natural world beyond conscious human purpose – a world that is created prior to man and develops according to its own internal dynamic; 'reality' is immutable, an overwhelming force that becomes reified as part of everyday 'common sense'. Once the subjective realm is disposed of in this way, faith in the predictability of human behaviour can be embraced with the passion of a religious cult. Thus, if through all of this, any revolutionary perspective whatsover remained, it consisted of accurately foreseeing the moment of historical transformation by analysing with precision the structural and behavioural tendencies at work in capitalist society. Gramsci saw in the growing Marxist emphasis upon scientific prediction a fatalistic delusion that undermined political initiative, as it did, for example, in both the reformist and orthodox wings of the Italian Socialist Party prior to 1920 and even in the PCI itself after the founding of the party in 1921. What theorists like Antonio Graziadei (Bukharin's counterpart in Italy) regarded as the Marxism appropriate to the new scientific-technological age, Gramsci attacked as a mystification of the political imperatives needed to be confronted in the struggle at hand. It was simply another way of reifying Marxist theory itself, of resolving practical tasks through 'scientific analysis':

> The situating of the problem as a search for laws and for constant, regular and uniform lines is connected to a need, conceived in a somewhat puerile and ingenious way, to resolve in preemptory fashion the practical problem of the predictability of historical events. . . . In reality one can foresee only the struggle, but not the concrete moments of the struggle, which can but be the results of opposing forces in continuous movement, which are never reduced to fixed qualities since within them quantity is continuously becoming quality. In reality one can 'foresee' to the extent that one acts, to the extent that one applies a voluntary effort and therefore contributes concretely to creating the result 'foreseen'. Prediction reveals itself thus not as a scientific act of knowledge, but as the abstract expression of the effort made, the practical way of creating a collective will.[11]

The 'future', then, can be nothing more than the application of human will to the historical material that is available; it is a complex interplay of subjective and objective forces. The preoccupation with prediction tends to block imaginative foresight by restricting political activity to a pre-conceived 'effective reality'. 'Only the man who wills something strongly can identify the elements which are necessary to the realization of his will', wrote Gramsci. Prediction 'precisely acquires that importance in the living brain of the individual who makes the prediction, and who by the strength of his will makes it come true'.[12] Without this element of political consciousness, prediction is nothing but the empty exercise of those whom Gramsci called 'byzantine theorists' – Marxists who value theory for its own sake, as a 'pastime' that has no action frame of reference.

For Gramsci, therefore, the only philosophical standpoint consistent with revolutionary Marxism was a conception of knowledge, ideas, and consciousness as both an expression of the material world and as a creative *transforming* agent – a dialectical notion that was a definite advance beyond the determinism of the positivists and formal theorists. Historical limitations can only be overcome through ongoing *political* activity (praxis), in the struggle for socialist transformation; at the same time, self-realization is achieved not through individual expressions of human will but as part of the collective political emancipation of the oppressed classes. Gramsci wanted to distinguish his own 'voluntarism', anchored in class analysis and historical understanding, from non-Marxist approaches like the fascist notion of 'volunteers' or Gentile's exaltation of the 'act', which viewed the self-conscious activity of a few leaders as a powerful causal force that could transcend historical conditions. To put it another way: 'Philosophy of the act, not of the "pure" act, but rather of the real "impure" act, in the most profane and worldly sense of the word.'[13]

Gramsci thus wanted to dispose of one of the most fashionable tenets of traditional Marxism − that human behaviour can be understood as a direct response to external stimuli, determined by social and economic conditions; and with this critique as a springboard, he was the first Marxist to insist upon the role of consciousness in shaping revolutionary change. As the *Prison Notebooks* repeatedly stressed, material forces acquire meaning only through human definition and engagement that includes a variety of possible mediations and individual perceptions. Ideas, concepts, the theoretical enterprise itself, are all part of an historically-evolving socio-political process and, as such, resist simple determinist models. Methods and techniques of analysis can serve little function independent of their historical content and purpose; social or political science in this sense can be nothing other than the 'critical' science of politically motivated persons who seek simultaneously to understand and change objective reality. For,

> the existence of objective conditions, of possibilities of freedom is not yet enough: it is necessary to 'know' them, and know how to use them. And to want to use them. Man, in this sense, is concrete will, that is, the effective application of the abstract will or vital impulse to the concrete means which realize such a will.[14]

In Gramsci's dialectical conception of history, then, we find a theory of human activity as shaped or 'determined' by social structures and which is also the subject, creator of new forms that challenge and overturn those same structures. As the oppressed strata reach awareness of limitations imposed by class society and struggle to redefine and transcend those limitations, they take the initiative and begin to move towards emancipation precisely as their needs, demands, perceptions expand and then explode beyond the old structural boundaries that have contained them for so long. Or, as Gramsci put it: 'Structure ceases to be an external force which crushes man, assimilates him to itself and makes him passive, and is transformed into a means of freedom, an instrument to create a new ethical political form and a source of new initiatives.'[15] In Hegelian terms, the transition from the realm of necessity to the realm of freedom must always be a *conscious*, self-actualizing process on the part of the oppressed, something the various forms of objectivist Marxism cannot comprehend, for they are locked into static categories. Gramsci often poked fun at the tendency to fetishize structures (the state, the mode of production) as if they were not created and held together by living, breathing human beings:

> Thus one could imagine a recruit explaining to the recruiting officers the theory of the state as superior to individuals and demanding that they should leave in liberty his physical and material person and just enroll that mysterious something that contributes to building that national something known as the state.'[16]

The Marxism that emerges from the pages of the *Prison Notebooks* can be defined as a *critical theory* that fuses elements of structure and consciousness, science and philosophy, subject and object – a conception which, however unsystematically formulated, is a marked advance upon what until the 1920s was the paradigm of orthodox Marxism. Theory functioned not to unravel the laws of nature but rather to provide new levels of historical consciousness for purposes of building a revolutionary movement. This new, reconstituted Marxism was aptly described by Gramsci as the 'philosophy of praxis' – conveying a vision of theory at once philosophical and political. The nexus philosophy-politics is a central theme of Gramsci's thought. It was the emancipatory role of philosophy, as the 'organizing' principle of a new moral-political order, to articulate and diffuse alternative ways of conceptualizing the world and to establish the foundation of a new language and sense of community among the 'subaltern' strata. Philosophy (and 'theory') in this definition is above all a creative political instrument that imparts unity, logic, and purpose to mass struggles, for it is precisely in this 'intellectual' arena that political conflict gets shaped. In other words, 'philosophy of praxis had two tasks to perform: to combat modern ideologies in their most refined form, in order to be able to constitute its own group of independent intellectuals; and to educate the popular masses, whose culture was medieval.'[17] Philosophy, as Gramsci viewed it, was a negating or dialectical form of thought, a more activating mode of discourse in that it constituted a transcendent (revolutionary) world-view in opposition to the established (or hegemonic) modes of thought and culture, including religion. 'Philosophy is criticism and the superseding of religion and "common sense"', precisely because neither religion nor common sense can ever provide the basis of a truly collective 'intellectual-moral' order, namely socialism.[18] For Gramsci, therefore, authentic (i.e. 'critical') philosophy was not to be abandoned or superseded as part of a scientific project, as the orthodox Marxists had suggested, but was to be a guiding part of the revolutionary process itself.[19]

But philosophy, precisely because it imparts conscious direction to political struggles, should not be confused with the detached and speculative thinking of the traditional philosophers (including theorists like Croce whom Gramsci criticized in much the same way Marx attacked Hegel). Ideas become important only when they can be translated into collective social and political forces. Hence:

> For a mass of people to be led to think coherently and in the same coherent fashion about the present world, is a 'philosophical' event far more important and 'original' than the discovery by some philosophical 'genius' of a truth which remains the property of a small group of intellectuals.[20]

It was such an elitist conception of philosophy, as Gramsci often stressed, that distinguished Catholicism from Marxism. The Church was always content to allow the oppressed masses to drift along in their ignorance and passivity, while the 'philosophy of praxis' seeks to establish an organic unity between intellectuals and the lower strata and 'does not tend to leave the "simple" in their primitive philosophy of common sense, but rather to lead them to a higher conception of life'.[21] Here Gramsci recognized that religious faith, much like the scientific spirit, tends to instil an apolitical fatalism among the oppressed and therefore must be combated as an anti-revolutionary ideology. The philosophy of a creative Marxism supplies the vital theoretical principles and concepts that shape peoples' struggle to challenge the oppression of everyday existence and overcome their sense of powerlessness; this is a good part of what is behind Gramsci's assertion that 'all men are philosophers'.[22]

As for Croce, Gramsci found his speculative and contemplative attitude towards theory antithetical to the active revolutionary spirit; what was missing from idealist philosophy was the practical, 'mundane' element so vital to Marxist praxis. Like Hegel, Croce had conceptualized historical development as the unfolding of self-consciousness, as creative human will overpowering the material world. Croce's analysis of nineteenth century Italy, for example, focused strictly upon the 'ethico-political' dialectic – in other words, transformations at the level of the superstructure. There were only passing allusions to material conditions, or to concrete social structures of any kind. Croce had in fact dismissed the materialist conception of history as a 'theological' approach that employed economics as a kind of 'hidden god'. Gramsci responded by saying that, while Croce's contribution in uncovering the ideological role of 'hegemony' or consensus in Italian politics was original and praiseworthy, his theory of history was in the final analysis abstract in that it completely overlooked the 'moment' of class struggle. As 'speculative history', it detached consciousness from material conditions, subject from object, and ended up treating the ethico-political realm 'as if it had just appeared from the blue'. It was thus Croce himself who had adopted a religious frame of mind:

> Croce is so involved in his own method and speculative language that these are the only standards he can use. When he writes that in the philosophy of praxis the structure is like a hidden god, this would hold good if the philosophy of praxis were speculative philosophy and not absolute historicism – an historicism that is completely free from all transcendental and theological vestiges.[23]

The unified philosophical perspective that emerges from the *Prison Notebooks* should be enough to dispel the accusations of 'voluntarism' and 'subjectivism' that have been made against Gramsci, not to mention the excessively idealist interpretations of this theory that stress its supposedly 'liberal' or 'open' qualities.[24] This both distorts Gramsci's revolutionary theory and negates the real significance of his contribution to the Marxist tradition. For what the 'philosophy of praxis' historically represents, above all, is precisely the supersession of the old divisions between philosophy, science, and politics that were traditionally characteristic of Western intellectual life, Marxism included, in favour of a new totalizing synthesis. Once this transcendence of the old 'metaphysical' categories of thought was achieved, as part of the general process of revolutionary transformation, subject and object could exist only in the form of a dialectical relationship:

> The philosophy of praxis is consciousness full of contradictions, in which the philosopher himself, understood both individually and as an entire social group, not merely grasps the contradictions, but posits himself as an element of the contradiction and elevates this element to a principle of knowledge and therefore of action.[25]

It is praxis rooted in the conception of totality, then, that activates the creative element in Marxism — a unique and original theory that opens up an entirely new phase of universal thought and socio-political change. In contrast to the mechanistic theorists of orthodox Marxism, who carried materialism to its objectivist extreme, Gramsci asserted that a *revolutionary* understanding of bourgeois society could proceed only from a philosophical base and ongoing political involvement; in contrast to the idealists like Croce and Sorel, who sought to graft onto Marxism 'alien' kinds of philosophies, Gramsci always insisted upon the autonomy of Marxism, which he considered to be not only self-sufficient but antagonistic to other world-views such as liberalism and Catholicism.[26] With these philosophical assumptions as a point of departure, let us turn now to a more concrete historical-political dimension of Gramsci's thought — the important concept of ideological hegemony.

2. Ideological Hegemony and Class Struggle

When 'scientific' Marxists stressed the role of objective conditions, or economic determinants, in the transition from capitalism to socialism, they assumed that politics, ideology, and culture could be understood as a reflection of the material 'base', as elements of the 'superstructure'. In this view subjectivity is regarded as mere 'appearance', with no independent or continuous existence of its own. Such a crude materialist interpretation of Marx helps to explain why so few Marxist theorists have been sensitive to the political role of ideologies and consciousness. It is a debilitating legacy that continues to obstruct the Marxist left even today. Gramsci emphatically rejected that approach, both in his early writings and in the *Prison Notebooks*, and stressed that it would be necessary to come to grips with the much more dynamic and complex relationship between base and superstructure; from this, he proceeded to formulate an alternative to the one-dimensionality of traditional Marxism that suggests a very different approach to the problem of revolutionary strategy.

Gramsci did not deny the primacy of the mode of production in shaping historical development over the long run, especially during periods of stability or slow evolutionary change, when the established order persisted more or less intact. But this framework, though useful for some purposes, somehow always failed to explain the vital *transformative* moments involving massive upheaval, conflict, and revolution, when one system was being superseded by something qualitatively new. In Gramsci's conception, the only truly *revolutionary* theory would be one that went beyond this economic determinism to take into account the concrete and rich interplay of diverse forces during 'conjunctural' periods of social transformation. Thus, instead of conceiving of the superstructure as a simple reflection of the economic base, Gramsci viewed the relationship as constantly changing and reciprocal in its historical complexity; politics, ideas, religion, and culture may not be autonomous in any 'ultimate' sense, but their causal power in any given transitional period could be overriding. The dynamic relationship of forces at work in any society during a particular time span should be investigated as sytematically as possible, rather than assumed in dogmatic fashion, or derived from a set of universally valid propositons. It follows that:

> The claim presented as an essential postulate of historical materialism, that every fluctuation of politics and ideology can be presented and expounded as an immediate expression of the structure [i.e. base], must be contested in theory as primitive infantilism, and combated in practice with the authentic testimony of Marx. . . .[1]

Any conceptual schema based upon the strict and unwavering determination of economic conditions would inevitably be undialectical and mechanical – devoid of historical and political content.

Beyond this general methodological statement, Gramsci argued that Marxism itself originated as a philosophical system (having evolved out of nineteenth century German idealism) and matured through the imperatives of historical research and political struggle. In other words, Marxist theory and practice itself initially gained expression within the realm of the superstructure. Moreover, in a number of places Gramsci approvingly referred to Marx's statement that human beings develop consciousness and become political actors on the ideological terrain in support of his premise that cultural, political, and ideological forms (including 'survivals' of previous epochs) shape the nature and outcome of revolutionary struggle. It is precisely these beliefs, attitudes, and even superstitions and myths that are most 'material' or 'real' in their capacity to inspire people towards action, that are catalysts in activating objective contradictions, which otherwise are nothing more than empty abstractions. Thus: 'To the extent that ideologies are historically necessary they have a validity which is "psychological"; they "organize" human masses and create the terrain on which men move, acquire consciousness of their position, struggle, etc.'[2] For Gramsci, contradictions do not 'explode' but rather are seized upon, grabbed hold of, actualized through the mental and psychic power of human beings.

To conceptualize this reciprocity between base and superstructure in terms of its impact upon class relations and political struggle, Gramsci introduced the notion of 'hegemony', or 'ideological hegemony' as it is often labelled. This is the basic theoretical point of departure for Gramsci's Marxism, including his theory of the party. The classical Marxist approach to power – including Lenin's own limited concept of hegemony – was one-sided in the exclusive attention it paid to the role of force and coercion as the basis of ruling class domination. In fact, as Max Weber noted in his analysis of bureaucracy, Marxism had typically ignored any form of domination outside the sphere of production itself. From Gramsci's perspective, what was missing was an understanding of the subtle but pervasive forms of ideological control and manipulation that served to perpetuate *all* repressive structures – a crippling analytical deficiency that held back the advance of political strategy in all previous socialist movements. Gramsci appeared to sense this problem quite clearly in some of his early writings and in his contribution to the 'Lyons' Theses' at the Third PCI Congress in 1926, but nowhere does he elaborate it theoretically until his prison writings. Throughout the *Prison Notebooks* Gramsci's overwhelming preoccupation was with the ideological dimension – an over-emphasis attributable no doubt to his self-conscious desire to correct the mechanical bias of conventional Marxist theory. Gramsci was originally influenced in this direction by Croce's idea of the 'ethico-political' as a leading theme of a particular stage of history – a concept not far removed from the notion of an epochal 'spirit' found in Montesquieu and Hegel, but transformed by Gramsci into an element of class domination and thus demystified of its abstract idealist trappings.

In differentiating two fundamental types of political control, Gramsci contrasted the functions of 'domination' (direct physical coercion) with those of 'hegemony' or 'direction' (consent, ideological control), which correspond roughly to the Hegelian distinction between political society and civil society,[3] He assumed that no regime, regardless of how authoritarian it was, could sustain itself primarily through organized state power; in the long run, its scope of popular support or 'legitimacy' was always bound to contribute to stability, particularly during times of stress or crisis. It was further obvious to

Gramsci that Marxism, as a theory striving towards universality, would have to take account of both spheres of authority in order to effectively press its political claims. By hegemony Gramsci meant the permeation throughout civil society — including a whole range of structures and activities like trade unions, schools, the churches, and the family — of an entire system of values, attitudes, beliefs, morality, etc. that is in one way or another supportive of the established order and the class interests that dominate it. Hegemony in this sense might be defined as an 'organizing principle', or world-view (or combination of such world-views), that is diffused by agencies of ideological control and socialization into every area of daily life. To the extent that this prevailing consciousness is internalized by the broad masses, it becomes part of 'common sense'; as all ruling elites seek to perpetuate their power, wealth, and status, they necessarily attempt to popularize their own philosophy, culture, morality, etc. and render them unchallengeable, part of the natural order of things. For hegemony to assert itself successfully in any society, therefore, it must operate in a dualistic manner: as a 'general conception of life' for the masses, and as a 'scholastic programme' or set of principles which is advanced by a sector of the intellectuals.[4]

Gramsci's analysis went much further than any previous Marxist theory to provide an understanding of why the European working class had on the whole failed to develop revolutionary consciousness and had instead moved towards reformism. Whereas the commonplace explanations had stressed the mechanical or fortuitous aspects of this crucial predicament — leadership 'betrayal', organization degeneration, or the absence of a sufficient crisis in capitalism — Gramsci looked for an answer in the subjective conditions of proletarian existence itself. Owing to the subordination of everyday life to bourgeois ideology, class struggle could not be expected to produce *socialist* consciousness spontaneously, regardless of the historical situation; the decline of the Second International could not be explained simply as an elite phenomenon, but would have to be explored to the very roots of the popular psyche itself. Where hegemony appeared as a strong force, it fulfilled a role that guns and tanks could never perform. It mystified power relations, public issues, and events;

it encouraged a sense of fatalism and passivity towards political action; and it justified every type of system-serving sacrifice and deprivation. In short, hegemony worked in many ways to induce the oppressed to accept or 'consent' to their own exploitation and daily misery.

But Gramsci never viewed the exercise of hegemony as something total or static; its scope and forms, and thus its specific impact, varied greatly from society to society and as such was always of uncertain proportions. Gramsci's approach to consciousness thus envisages a dynamic historical dimension that is missing from Lukacs' all-encompassing notion of reification, according to which every aspect of social relations in bourgeois society takes on the character of relations between commodities. If for Lukacs reified consciousness was the inevitable expression of an expanding market structure under capitalism that destroyed the subjectivity of the proletariat in its totalistic sweep, for Gramsci hegemony was always a matter of the degree of equilibrium that obtains between state and civil society. This correspondence between political institutions and the popular ideologies that support them may be either stable or precarious – a factor that, owing to the peculiarities of historical development in a given society, determines the consensual 'resources' that ruling groups may be able to mobilize at times of crisis. A number of variables are involved here, including the capacity of dominant elites to manipulate attitudes, values, and life-styles through media, education, culture, language, etc. – a capacity which has been highly refined only in the advanced industrial societies of the twentieth century. In fact, Gramsci found that *disequilibrium* rather than ideological stability was the rule for most of European history.

The two-dimensional conception of political domination that Gramsci outlined in the *Prison Notebooks* leads to an important strategic proposition: that any crisis of the established order which might open the way to revolutionary transformation must follow a crisis of ideological hegemony in civil society – i.e. the undermining of traditional social and authority relations, cultural patterns, and lifestyles that in most cases would involve an organic, long-range struggle between 'competing systems'. The main political task of a socialist movement then is to create a 'counter-hegemony' to break the ideological bond between the ruling class and various sectors of the general population. In this process, structural and ideological change would have to occur as part of the same overall struggle; and yet the ideological transformations that set the stage for direct power confrontations are not simply reflections of changes in the material base. To the extent that the position of the ruling class would have to be demystified at the level of popular beliefs before the armed struggle for state power became meaningful, value-conflicts could no longer be dismissed by Marxists as illusory or mere phantoms but would have to be recognized as concrete political forces that shape the nature of class struggle. According to Gramsci, the 'crisis of the modern state' occurs when the ruling class is 'stripped of its spiritual prestige and power' and reduced to its 'economic-corporate' existence, which reveals more clearly than ever the real cause of oppression.[5] A crisis of this sort may occur when

> the ruling class has failed in some major political undertaking for which, it has requested, or forcibly extracted, the consent of the broad masses (war, for example), or because the huge masses . . . have passed suddenly from a state of political passivity to a certain activity, and put forward demands which taken together . . . add up to a revolution.[6]

At the same time, Gramsci realized that the erosion of ideological hegemony created only the *possibilities* for advancing towards socialism; demystifying the old consciousness did not inevitably bring with it new forms of revolutionary consciousness. Moreover, the new 'integrated culture' would probably not emerge full-blown out of an ideological vacuum but should be expected to advance by stages, initially taking the form of scepticism, doubting, and cynicism about prevailing ideas, theories, and values, as well as sporadic manifestations of primitive revolt. The periods of upheaval are themselves still shaped by the contradictions of class society. Thus:

> If the ruling class has lost its consensus, i.e. is no longer 'leading' but only 'dominant', exercising coercive force alone, this means precisely

that the great masses have become detached from their traditional ideologies, and no longer believe what they used to believe previously, etc. The crisis consists precisely in the fact that the old is dying and the new cannot be born; in this interregnum a great variety of morbid symptoms appears.[7]

What matters here, as Gramsci often pointed out, is the capacity of the left to step into the vacuum and take advantage of new historical possibilities, which in turn depends upon intellectual-cultural preparation, level of organization, and unity ('homogeneity') of the revolutionary movement. Not only must the old meanings and norms of everyday life be destroyed, but new ones must be constructed in their place. Hence the struggle for ideological hegemony has two phases: to penetrate the false world of established appearances rooted in the dominant belief systems and to create an entirely new universe of ideas and values that would provide the basis for human liberation.

Gramsci's concept of hegemony introduces fundamentally new insights into the issue of political domination within the Marxist tradition, and consequently opens up new strategic perspectives — including a redefinition of the function of the revolutionary party (see Chapter 5 below). Up to this point, the problematic of hegemony has been viewed as *form*, as a general aspect of authority and legitimacy in class society. But what of the specific historical content of hegemony, its peculiar manifestations, in particular societies? What is its role in the advanced capitalist societies of Western Europe and North America? True to his strongly historical orientation, Gramsci never failed to bring his own theoretical generalizations down to earth, and his concrete analysis of hegemony leads him to a number of very suggestive propositions. In the *Prison Notebooks*, Gramsci examined a wide range of ideological forces: religion (especially Catholicism), nationalism, the family, technology, unique historical traditions, and even individual great thinkers like Croce.[8] Though his primary focus was Italy, Gramsci devoted much attention to other national experiences in countries like France, Germany, England, Russia, and the United States.

In the Italian context, it was the powerful ideological and cultural influence of the Church and Catholicism, which had been much less undermined by the secular thrust of liberalism and industrialization than in France and elsewhere, that shaped class conflict in a unique way. Though it was obvious that the vast majority of Italians, including industrial workers, accepted religious faith and the traditional life-styles that were rooted in it, Marxists had always assumed that Catholicism would wither away as the by-product of the struggle against capitalism. Gramsci was the first to insist that religion as a hegemonic ideology would have to be confronted within the context of transforming popular consciousness as both the *pre-condition* to abolishing capitalism and a central aspect of liberation itself. The Church in Italy was not merely part of the institutional *status quo*, a privileged bastion of economic wealth and social status; nor was Catholicism strictly a metaphysical set of beliefs. Religious ideology performed a concrete political function in containing and distorting popular rebellion, for example by stressing the 'natural' (God-given) character of existing structures such as private property and the family, the importance of transcendental commitment over everyday ('earthly') collective action to change the world, the supposed moral virtues of poverty and weakness, and the sacrosanct nature of all forms of established authority. Gramsci also emphasized that the Church hierarchy, by setting itself off from the general population as an ecclesiastical caste, reinforced the ignorance, passivity, and provincialism that had always been the lot of the popular strata under feudalism. Since Italy had been the traditional geographical locus of the Roman Empire and the Vatican, the norms of Catholicism were all the more powerful and the need to combat them directly all the more crucial.

In other societies, such as England, the Netherlands, and the United States, Protestantism emerged as the hegemonic religious ideology, but Gramsci evaluated its impact in different terms from that of Catholicism – along the lines of Max Weber's thesis in *The Protestant Ethic and the Spirit of Capitalism*. Whereas Catholicism, as the dominant belief system of pre-industrial Europe, embraced an 'otherworldly' kind of conservatism, the puritanism that came out of the Reformation had been closely linked to the rise of the bourgeoisie, with its commitment to the temporal values of hard work, thrift and frugality, sacrifice, self-discipline, etc. Earthly achievements and good deeds became the measure of religious salvation, in accordance with the notion of predestination; such values made up the core consciousness of an emerging capitalist society, with its dependence upon efficiency and productivity, upon machine technology and bureaucracy. Gramsci observed that the Protestant ethic was more universally assimilated by the popular masses in the United States than elsewhere, owing to the absence of feudal remnants (such as an established Church) and to the more advanced levels of industrial development. Indeed, as he suggested in 'Americanism and Fordism' (written in 1931), the strong puritanical regulation of moral-personal life helped to create in the US an historically new type of individual – the 'trained gorilla' so totally submerged in the rationalized work process that pleasure, sensuality, and critical thinking could be expressed in only the most restrictive (and often guilt-ridden) manner.[9]

Though Gramsci nowhere formulates a theory of the family and sexuality, he does produce some insights into the nexus puritanism-capitalism-family that were paralleled within Marxism only by the pioneering work of Wilhelm Reich. Gramsci argued that the stabilization of sexual relations within the monogamous family, with the full support of religious dogma behind it, was central to creating a work force that is efficient and obedient. In this sense the family constitutes the basic social unit of civil society, and puritanism is its underlying ideological justification. As capitalism expands and increases its reliance upon technology and bureaucratic structures, 'these new methods demand a rigorous discipline of the sexual instincts . . . and with it a strengthening of the "family" in a wide sense and of the regulation and stability of sexual relations'. Thus, the repressed sexuality that is the outgrowth of the nuclear family operates to restrict psychically the worker both within and outside the workplace: 'It seems clear that the new industrialism wants monogamy: it wants the man as worker not to squander his nervous energies in the disorderly and stimulating pursuit of occasional sexual satisfaction. The employee who goes to work after a night of "excess" is no good for his work.'[10] It would not be surprising, therefore, to find that the most progressive approaches to sex and morality tend to come from those groups furthest removed from the production process; nor would it be surprising, Gramsci suggests, to discover that women's struggle against patriarchal oppression inevitably activates new patterns of thought and behaviour that help to undermine bourgeois hegemony within the workplace itself.

Gramsci devoted even more attention to the role of bureaucracy and technology as sources of a new hegemonic ideology specific to the advanced capitalist countries, especially the United States, where these forces were beginning to create the foundations of a 'new industrialism'. Consistent with its previous economist biases, Marxism had generally dismissed bureaucracy as a problem to be confronted at all, or had viewed it as the simple expression of bourgeois class interests. Though Marx himself could hardly be accused of this theoretical deficiency, writing as he did well before the age of large-scale organization (in both private *and* public realms), its legacy continued well into the twentieth century and helped to retard a revolutionary understanding of what may be the most significant co-optative mechanism in late capitalism. It was no coincidence that Weber and Robert Michels, the two theorists who first analysed bureaucracy as a new form of domination in bourgeois society, were not Marxists; nor was it surprising that their conception of organization as an autonomous social force met with harsh criticism from Marxists of all tendencies. Writing as a liberal, Weber saw in technology and bureaucracy the basis of a new rationality that was the logical and irreversible product of industrialization in any context. Bureaucratic structures were the unavoidable outgrowth of the capitalist demand for higher and higher levels of productivity. They brought increasingly centralized modes of authority and planning, a highly-specialized division of labour, and, what is perhaps most crucial, a source of new legitimacy for the bourgeoisie itself. What the latter meant for Weber was the development of a 'rational-legal' culture that permeated all spheres of society: emphasis upon instrumental norms, the domain of law and routine procedures of work, professionalization, obedience to authority, impersonal social relations, etc. The impact of all this was to rationalize the instruments of domination available to political elites while at the same time rendering the general population loyal, fragmented, and depoliticized. Michels argued essentially the same thesis in his book *Political Parties* (written in 1911, before the main thrust of Weber's work), but he applied it to the more specific problem of the decline of German Social Democracy before the First World War. What is most important about both Weber and Michels is that they saw in bureaucracy as a *political* phenomenon the defining motif of twentieth century capitalism.

Gramsci saw more or less the same tendencies at work, but he understood them as part of his revolutionary approach to the problem of ideological hegemony. As elements of the new rationality, bureaucracy and technology were not so much irreversible forces of industrialization as sources of cultural-intellectual-ideological domination that obscured class and power relations, and which would have to be directly confronted and reshaped in the course of socialist transformation. Gramsci was concerned above all about the destructive influence of new techniques such as 'scientific management' in industry, or Taylorism, upon the class consciousness of workers; as he pointed out in 'Americanism and Fordism', the growing rationalization of capitalism coincided with both the consolidation of capitalism and the rise of fascism in Europe between the wars. What Weber had analysed was correct so far as the evolution of capitalism was concerned, but it lacked a dialectical vision of possible further change; it accepted bureaucratization as inevitable. Gramsci shared Weber's main generalizations, but integrated them into a theory of class struggle. Within Marxism, he was among the first to anticipate the transition from classical competitive capitalism to the highly-organized state-corporate economy, particularly in terms of its effect upon popular consciousness. What seemed to sensitize Gramsci to this epochal change was in part his theory of hegemony, in part the actual emergence of fascism in Italy during the twenties.

Gramsci's fragmentary but original insights into bureaucratic and technological rationality constitute in some ways a preliminary statement to Marcuse's later *One-Dimensional Man*.[11] While the time span here is a full generation, Gramsci had clearly foreseen in Taylorism a hegemonic ideological force in advanced capitalism equivalent to the religious systems during feudalism and early capitalism. The new pragmatic and secular 'theology' of advancing industrialization arose from a foundation of science, technology, and organization – with basically the same bourgeois infrastructure and class relations still intact. Gramsci projected that the relationalization of work and production would create a 'collective man' (with American capitalism already a model) who would passively perform everyday tasks and who would accept a suffocating conformism that resulted from the standardization of thought and action. (Marcuse's 'one-dimensionality'?) Like Catholicism, puritanism, and patriarchal ideology, technological rationality enforces psychic repression and contributes to the development of authoritarian personality characteristics. Gramsci pointed to Taylorism in the US and the fascist corporate state in Italy as harbingers of the most sophisticated mode of capitalist domination, in which the workers would be totally subordinated to machine specialization and the cult of efficiency. The diffusion of bureaucratic-technological norms would mean the destruction of all intellectual, artistic, and even human content to production and, in the end, the grinding down of the workers' life to virtual nothingness. By reducing the workers to obedient automatons, rationalization would undermine creative and critical thinking and break down the impulse to resist exploitation. Gramsci saw in Henry Ford, for example, the innovative corporate magnate who quickly perceived new opportunities for increasing productivity by regulating the complete moral-psychological being of the worker. The ultimate goal was to create a routinized psychic structure for work under capitalism so that, as Gramsci put it: 'The new type of worker will be a repetition, in different form, of peasants in the villages.'[12]

To the extent, then, that the new rationalized capitalism served to reinforce false consciousness among the oppressed strata, it followed that Marx's propositions concerning the intensification of class struggle with advanced economic development might have to be seriously re-examined. It also suggested that *ideological* domination rather than direct political coercion had become the primary instrument of bourgeois rule – a generalization that may help to explain the subtle but effective assimilation of the proletariat in the post-Second

World War period. Gramsci stressed that the problematic of ideological hegemony took on a greater importance in the more developed countries, since the equilibrium between state and civil society tended to be much stronger than in transitional or primarily agrarian countries like pre-revolutionary Russia. This idea has many implications for political strategy. Gramsci's argument here is that the growing complexity of civil society in advanced capitalism (the development of a skilled labour force, the importance of knowledge and education in production, the role of the mass media, the availability of more sophisticated techniques of ideological control, the penetration of civil society by the state, etc.) could only mean that authority and power would have to be viewed in a broader context than, for example, was the case under Russian conditions:

> In Russia the state was everything, civil society was primordial and gelatinous; in the West, there was a proper relation between state and civil society, and when the state trembled a sturdy structure of civil society was at once revealed. The state was only an outer ditch, behind which there stood a powerful system of fortresses and earthworks: more or less numerous from one state to the next, it goes without saying – but this precisely necessitated an accurate reconnaissance of each individual country.[13]

As historical examples of fragile hegemony, where the authority of the ruling classes rested upon very shaky ideological foundations, Gramsci referred to nineteenth century Germany and to the whole history of Italy from the Renaissance on. In the first instance, Gramsci saw German intellectual and cultural life as limited to a small nucleus of elites who had virtually no contact with the masses. The ideological influence of these narrow groups of intellectuals, artists, and politicians was so contained that it never appeared as an organic part of popular consciousness; the masses therefore moved more freely on their own, without any all-embracing *Weltanschauung* or 'organizing principle' diffused from above. Given the subsequent lack of German national unity, no larger sense of community could develop to the point of providing consensus of either the feudal aristocracy or the emergent bourgeoisie. Without any real 'organic or disciplinary bonds' linking the antagonistic classes together, ideological domination became 'merely a phenomenon of abstract cultural influence', thus making necessary at some time the exercise of more coercive methods of rule to counter political instability or mobilize popular support for particular objectives.[14] This dynamic of German development continued well into the twentieth century, though Gramsci's analysis does not take account of the Bismarck period, Weimar, and the rise of Nazism.

Gramsci contrasted this dynamic with the Reformation, the bearer of which was the great mass of German people rather than a detached intellectual-political elite. He made the same kinds of comparisons between the Renaissance and the French Revolution. The Renaissance had nourished a thriving cultural, social, and political life, but it was almost totally divorced from the everyday existence of the general population; it was mainly limited to a 'restricted intellectual aristocracy', or 'courtly circles', in Croce's words. The ideological forces set in motion by the Renaissance, though powerful, were self-contained and failed to create a lasting equilibrium between state and civil society. The French Revolution, on the other hand, burst upon the scene as a profoundly *mass* phenomenon – a 'national-popular' movement that generated a cohesive political element for the French people.[15] To be sure, this Jacobin thrust from above had its coercive and authoritarian movement, but once the broad linkage between elites and popular strata, town and countryside, was achieved the basis of a 'national-popular' community had been established. This was never really achieved in Germany or Italy.

In the case of Italy, Gramsci observed that – aside from the omnipresent influence of Catholicism – ideological hegemony, as a shared system of values that provided widespread legitimacy to dominant institutions and interests, was never well-developed. From at least the time of Machiavelli, when the stirrings of national unification first appeared, Italy had experienced sharp socio-political fragmentation and cleavage: divisions among the various city-states, between religious and anti-clerical interests, between North and South, between industrial capitalism and feudal agrarianism. Civil society lacked the cohesion that had developed in England, the United States, and even France, where a sense of national 'spirit' had accompanied the bourgeois revolution. The *Risorgimento* of the 1860s and 1870s, whatever its pretensions and goals as the prime mover of Italian unification, failed to establish an ideological bond between elites and popular strata that would make possible an extensive national community. The new ruling class, based mainly in the Piedmont, set out to 'conquer' Italy and managed to 'dominate' its political life, but it was never able to 'lead' or mobilize consent; as such, Northern liberalism became a 'dictatorship without hegemony', the expression of an unfulfilled bourgeois-democratic revolution.[16]

Gramsci went on to suggest that this disequilibrium created the conditions of perpetual political instability characterized by conflict and rivalry between personal factions and cliques having little mass constituency. During the three decades before the First World War this resulted in the 'decapitation' of socialist or working-class movements by the co-optation of their leadership elements into established oligarchical structures—a process known as *trasformismo*. What in effect occurred was a phenomenon that Gramsci labelled 'passive revolution': social and economic change presided over by the traditional ruling elites who were able to maintain their precarious political and cultural supremacy. As the subversive forces became absorbed, the ideological distinctions between 'left' and 'right' grew more and more blurred. Thus in the Italian situation class conflict was blunted by the fact that solidarity between *all* leadership elements became more intense than the bonds between *any* group of leaders and *any* given popular constituency.[17] Though for a period of time this vast disjuncture between state and civil society functioned to contain revolutionary insurgency in Italy, as it did in Russia, its long-range consequences were bound to be very explosive for the system, as post-First World War events were to demonstrate.

At the other extreme, Gramsci cited the United States as the best example of a society in which the ruling classes had historically established almost complete ideological hegemony. He argued that the unique success of American capitalism could be explained by the absence of a feudal stage of development; the first Anglo-Saxon pioneers who settled America brought with them a new 'moral energy', a 'new level of civilization', untrammelled by residues of the pre-industrial past, that provided the basis for the development of a unified capitalist economic system, politics, and culture. The dynamic new ideas that were transplanted onto fresh terrain assumed a certain rhythm and momentum of their own, whereas in Europe class struggle tended to fit the Marxist model. With no feudal restraints, the obstacles to capitalist development in the United States were more easily overcome than in most European countries. As Gramsci put it, 'The nonexistence of viscous parasitic sedimentations left behind by past phases of history has allowed industry, and commerce in particular, to develop on a sound basis.'[18] He observed that the early American settlers were the

> ... protagonists of the political and religious struggles in England, defeated but not humiliated or laid low in their country of origin. They import into America ... apart from moral energy and energy of the will, a certain level of civilization, a certain stage of European historical evolution, which, when transplanted by such men into the virgin soil of America, continues to develop the forces implicit in its nature but with an incomparably more rapid rhythm than in Old Europe, where there exists a whole series of checks (moral, intellectual, political, economic, incorporated in specific sections of the population, relics of past regimes which refuse to die out) which generate opposition to speedy progress and give to every initiative the equilibrium of mediocrity, diluting it in time and space.[19]

To understand American society it is necessary to realize that the whole life of the country has always revolved around capitalist production, from which has emerged a new type of human being, a new work process, a new national, material culture with no real feudal 'survivals' (e.g. a large peasantry) and, ultimately, a weak socialist tradition in comparison with other capitalist systems. Moreover, insofar as the particular way of life characteristic of liberal capitalism is related to the methods of production in the US, the unique strength of bourgeois hegemony facilitated the very kind of corporate rationality already mentioned; indeed, Gramsci often appeared to be saying that liberalism and technological rationality are simply different ideological components of the phenomenon 'Americanism'. Both were accepted as 'natural' to the US. The solid equilibrium between state and civil society in America meant that class conflict never became as politicized as it did in Europe, where large mass-based socialist movements developed to contest capitalist domination. In the US, opposition was historically confined to the economic realm and to the established two-party system by the rather imposing boundaries of liberal hegemony. In this context, revolutionary appeals rarely met with great success among workers and other oppressed groups such as blacks, while Marxism itself was seen as an 'alien' world-view adhered to only by utopian day-dreamers and eccentrics. With but few isolated exceptions, dissent and rebellion have never challenged the fundamental structures and values of bourgeois society in America.[20]

Gramsci's concept of ideological hegemony, rooted in a comprehensive philosophical-theoretical critique of classical Marxism, suggests new ways of thinking about political domination and, by extension, the crucial question of revolutionary strategy. A basic premise underlying Gramsci's approach is built around the distinction between 'organic' and 'conjunctural' aspects of struggle, which is roughly equivalent to the dichotomy between 'war of position' and 'war of movement' that will be examined more extensively in Chapter 5 below. What it signifies is the epochal struggle for ideological supremacy and 'leadership' (*direzione*) that must take place in the realm of civil society before the issue of state domination can ever be resolved. Gramsci sometimes compared the transition from capitalism to socialism with the long period of cultural and intellectual ferment that preceded and accompanied the Protestant Reformation as it arose out of Catholicism and the Roman Empire, and with the bourgeois overthrow of the *ancien regime* that was facilitated by the ideas of the Enlightenment. The destruction of the old institutions was seen by Gramsci as but a single moment in the vast historical modification of socio-political forces that occurs 'underneath the surface' of formal institutions. The ideological erosion of the bourgeois order at every level – economic, political, cultural, social – would precede the initiation of direct 'frontal assaults' on the state; this process would occur through the continuous and organic development of the subaltern or oppressed classes, which do not progress harmoniously but which surge ahead and suffer setbacks, come together and break up, move towards a variety of formations in response to specific influences and events, etc. Hence Gramsci's first priority was the multidimensional transformation of civil society, which he considered the ultimate key to the 'war of movement', since 'there can and must be a "political hegemony" even before the attainment of power'.[21]

What emerges from this overall strategic perspective is the conception of Marxism as a new 'integrated culture' pressing on all fronts to generate new historical possibilities, asserting as it grows an original culture, system of social relations, and economic order. For Gramsci, socialist transformation was more a *process* than an *event* or series of events. It involved above all the role of a negating consciousness in shaping particular demands, in 'structuring' the revolutionary situation itself, in defining mass responses to issues and actions, and in setting the contours of future ('post-revolutionary') development. Education – authentic political education – would be important, therefore, in combating the old mystifying beliefs and diffusing a socialist 'counter-hegemony' among all potentially revolutionary subjects; but it would be an education rooted in praxis, closely bound up with everyday political struggle.

In what was one of Gramsci's major insights, he projected that ideological encounters with the ruling class (the 'war of position') would take on an added importance with advancing stages of capitalist development. Whereas the Leninist focus on the 'conjunctural', or 'war of movement', was in some respects successful in the case of Tsarist Russia, where 'the state was everything and civil society nothing', a new strategy would be needed in the West to take account of the greater ideological 'entrenchment' of the bourgeoisie, where 'civil society has become a very complex structure and one which is resistant to the catastrophic "incursions" of the immediate economic element (crisis, depressions, etc.)'. Under these conditions of strengthened hegemony, 'a crisis cannot give the attacking forces the ability to organize with lightning speed in time and in space' and 'still less can it endow them with fighting spirit'.[22] Gramsci approvingly cited Trotsky's distinction between 'Eastern' and 'Western' fronts, noting that the former had fallen suddenly (i.e. Russia) while the latter would involve a longer and more complex struggle prior to the actual conquest of power. It followed that the fashionable Marxist schema (accepted by Lenin no less than by the theorists of the Second International) of a 'catastrophic' rupture that would permit the intervention of an organized revolutionary force would have to be abandoned in favour of a more organic, 'counter-hegemonic' strategy.

3. Mass Consciousness and Revolution

Classical Marxism failed adequately to confront, let alone resolve, the problem of revolutionary consciousness. This was to be expected, given its theoretical preoccupation with the mode of production, or economic 'base', as the determining factor in historical development. The totality of socialist transformation itself – including the vision of a qualitatively new society that embraces the ultimate goals of political struggle and the subjective foundations of a new world-view – was scarcely discussed before Lenin, and even within contemporary Marxism one finds the tendency to reduce 'superstructural' elements to their material context. Some of this one-sidedness seems to emerge from Marx's own writings, in which consciousness was implicitly seen as the imminent product of the changing internal dynamics of capitalism, with socialism growing organically out of the womb of bourgeois society. The basic premise of nineteenth-century Marxism was that the contradiction between wage labour and capital would lead inexorably to proletarian transcendence of the mature capitalist system; Marx often appeared to be saying that the oppressive conditions of existence under capitalism would suffice to impel the working class towards full socialist consciousness, with the everyday struggle for survival in class society itself providing the 'school' for revolution. Beyond this vague perspective on the complex issue of how socialist transformation would occur Marx never went, nor did he ever systematically examine the origins and nature of *differing* kinds of working-class consciousness. This omission, while understandable in the context of Marx's priorities, opened the door to the materialist vulgarization of Marxism typified by the late Engels and the theorists of the Second International, who saw in the problematic of consciousness nothing but a retrograde 'bourgeois idealism'.

Historically, such theoretical one-dimensionality could only produce the kind of shallow political strategy that was to lead European socialist movements into one failure after another. Marxism was either hemmed in by the empirical categories, concepts, and methods of scientific theory or restricted to the momentary practicalities of economic struggle; it lacked altogether any real subjective component, any social psychology of revolution, and thus any popular mobilizing power. Such a paralysing intellectual deficiency, revealed most clearly during moments of profound crisis, originated out of a crude mechanistic psychology that explained human behaviour primarily as a function of economic needs. It was one of Marx's real contributions to give theoretical meaning to this previously neglected factor, but in the later formulations of Marxism the economic took on the character of totality. Feelings, moods, ideas, values, aesthetics were viewed as irrational (i.e. 'subjective' or 'idealist'), while the true purpose of theory was to supply a rational-cognitive understanding of history, to present a coherent class analysis of bourgeois society. Great intellectual energy was committed to the task of discovering new knowledge about the laws of capitalist development; while often valuable in itself, from a *political* perspective the knowledge obtained from this enterprise was incomplete. Hence, when structural breakdown did occur in countries like Germany and Italy – when the objective conditions were, so to speak, 'ripe' for revolutionary upheaval – and when the masses seemed to be prepared for anti-capitalist mobilization, Marxists were not theoretically equipped to take advantage of the opportunities and wound up ceding the whole terrain of popular ideological struggle to the bourgeoisie (and to the fascists).

The crucial fact was that vast sectors of the proletariat (not to mention the peasantry and petty bourgeoisie) never adopted socialist politics in any meaningful sense but were, on the contrary, moving rapidly in the direction of reaction. The working class, far from having emerged as a class 'for itself', came increasingly under the spell of bourgeois-fascist ideological hegemony during the 1920s as capitalist consolidation assumed more harshly authoritarian forms. As Wilhelm Reich observed at the time, the fatal weakness of the left was its failure to create a 'mass psychology' that would permit it to 'speak the language of the broad masses' with imagination and emotional appeal. Marxism tended to be too schematic and abstract, too preoccupied with analyses of objective conditions:

> While we presented the masses with superb historical analyses and economic treatises on the contradictions of imperialism, Hitler stirred the deepest roots of their emotional being. As Marx would have put it, we left the praxis of the subjective factor to the idealists; we acted like mechanistic economistic materialists.[1]

Reich's point was that, despite the intense spirit of rebellion among the German people during the 1920s and early 1930s, 'socialism' never became a concrete vision for them, never became internalized, whereas 'fascism' became deeply psychic because it captured the emotional (and even 'romantic') sentiments of everyday life.

Reich criticized European Marxism for having lost touch of the needs, desires, fears, and anxieties of the masses in its singular search for knowledge of the contradictions of capitalism. What happened was that theory had projected an artificial and incorrect understanding of socio-political processes onto the consciousness of the oppressed classes, thus falling into the trap of an inverted form of 'subjective idealism', or what Lukacs called 'abstract utopianism'.[2] Having lost sight of the real nature of popular consciousness, the theorists and leaders of Marxist movements never realized that revolution, in any authentic sense, must spring from the politicization of all aspects of everyday life; there was no 'ready'made class consciousness' that simply evolved from the objective position of the proletariat itself. As Reich viewed the revolutionary process, the destruction of old institutions could occur only as part of transforming the basic psychological underpinnings that held them together. Class struggle must be conceptualized in the first instance as an ideological confrontation:

> We make and change the world only through the mind of man, through his will for work, his longing for happiness, in brief, through his psychological existence. The 'Marxists' who degenerated into 'economists' forgot this a long time ago. A global economic and political policy, if it means to create and secure international socialism, must find a point of contact with trivial, banal, primitive, simple every-day life, with the desires of the broadest masses . . . Only in this way

can the objective sociological process become one with the subjective consciousness of men and women, abolishing the contradiction and distance between the two.[3]

Reich's perceptive insights here parallel Gramsci's analyses of the Italian situation in the twenties and thirties, and indeed anticipate Gramsci's brilliant treatment of the problem of revolutionary consciousness in the *Prison Notebooks*. But Gramsci laid the foundations of his theory much earlier, even before the *Ordine Nuovo* period, when the influence of Croce upon him was particularly strong. Like Rosa Luxemburg in Germany, Gramsci rebelled against the narrow conception of politics advanced by Social Democracy in Italy and suggested, well before the rise of fascism, that the PSI could never prevail so long as it ignored the issue of consciousness and ideological struggle. In retrospect, Gramsci's Marxism belongs to the period of the 'Hegelian revival' that accompanied the disintegration of classical Marxism after the First World War – a crucial turning point that spans the Bolshevik Revolution, the collapse of the Second International, the emergence of fascist regimes in Europe, and, finally, the Stalinist deformation of Soviet politics and the Comintern. The traditional Marxist movements had failed to penetrate bourgeois hegemony, thus necessitating a whole new theoretical construction that could incorporate an active, dialectical perspective. The initial stirrings in this direction appeared even prior to the war, in the work of Antonio Labriola, in Lenin, and most visibly in Rosa Luxemburg. Gramsci's contribution begins as early as 1916, but it was not until the 1920s that this 'Hegelianized' Marxism was finally successful in cutting through the intellectual perimeters of the orthodoxy. This period of theoretical upheaval which matured for the most part *after* the political upheavals generated some important new tendencies: Karl Korsch and the 'ultra left' in Germany, the Council Communists, the work of Georg Lukacs, Reich and the sex-pol movement, and the first contributions of the 'Frankfurt School'. It is as part of this historical reconstitution of European Marxism that the political thought of Gramsci must be understood.

Gramsci's main premise was that revolutionary struggle, especially in its beginning stages, is more than anything else an *ideological* process. The political consciousness that defines any movement is shaped by the gradual and diffuse flow of ideas and life-experiences, involving an organic fusion of the 'personal' and 'cultural' realms with the political. The following passage reveals Gramsci's thinking during his early formative years:

> Man is above all else mind, consciousness – that is, he is a product of history, not nature. There is no other way of explaining why socialism has not come into existence already, although there have always been exploiters and exploited, creators of wealth and selfish consumers of wealth. Man has only been able to acquire a sense of his worth bit by bit, in one sector of society after another . . . And such awareness was not generated out of brute physiological needs, but out of intelligent reasoning, first of all by a few and later by entire social classes who perceived the causes of certain social facts and understood that there might be ways of converting the structure of repression into one of rebellion and social reconstruction. This means that every revolution has been preceded by an intense labour of social criticism, of cultural penetration and diffusion.[4]

Unfortunately, the Marxist movements of postwar Italy possessed none of Gramsci's insights into the revolutionary process, or if they did they clearly failed to apply them. Gramsci often criticized the Italian Socialist Party leadership for its failure to take advantage of the crisis of bourgeois authority in the years 1918–1920. Instead of supplying political and strategic direction during the wide-spread anti-capitalist insurrections of that critical period, the PSI was enslaved by the paralysis of its short-range economic goal-orientation on the one hand and its fatalistic waiting for the appearance of 'ripe' objective conditions on the other. Reformism and scientism were two sides of the same coin. The divorce between theory and practice within the PSI widened as the party leadership became obsessed with developing a 'correct line', assuming that the Italian working class would follow a valid analysis; there was correspondingly little effort to activate the masses by pursuing an imaginative strategy that could engage their subjective feelings, attitudes, and beliefs.[5] Gramsci saw in the gulf that separated the bureaucratized PSI directorate (and the trade union structure) from the workers the source of an institutionalized form of class collaboration that ultimately helped to pave the way to fascism. Lacking any organic, popular strategy, the PSI increasingly looked to the bourgeois state itself to solve the crisis of social life in Italy; the internal contradiction of a deradicalized party pushed it towards a 'counter-revolutionary' position that helped to restore capitalist order. For Gramsci, a major theoretical root of this dynamic of deradicalization was the one-sided understanding of Marxism itself – namely its failure to take up the problematic of consciousness.[6]

One example of the PSI's myopic approach to popular mobilization often cited by Gramsci was the narrow-minded rejection of certain widely-held cultural attitudes known as Futurism. Although a number of tendencies within Futurism represented progressive attacks upon the old culture (especially the Italian academic establishment) and were understood by many intellectuals and workers to be part of the general struggle against bourgeois society, Marxists in the PSI contemptuously ignored Futurism after declaring that it lacked socialist political content. Gramsci saw in it something vastly different: an ideological struggle that was calling into question a broad realm of cherished values (notably religion itself), as expressed through poetry, drama, painting, ballet, literature, etc. If the leading exponents of Futurism such as Marinetti did not define themselves as 'revolutionary' or 'Marxist' in the strict sense, they were nonetheless 'preparing new ground' in the overall struggle against bourgeois-Catholic civilization. Gramsci stressed that proletarian revolution would have to sweep away every component of the old order – the *cultural* as well as the economic and political. If socialism is to assert its ideological hegemony, it must create its own culture (i.e. its own popular poetry, drama, painting, ballet, literature) as an integral part of a total revolutionary process; in doing so, it must build upon embryonic currents of cultural protest and revolt. The Futurists, as Gramsci viewed them in the early period before they drifted towards fascism, embodied a counter-hegemonic potential that was never mobilized by the PSI.[7]

The *Ordine Nuovo* movement in Turin during 1919–1921 represented for Gramsci a pioneering attempt to construct a real alternative to the ossified Marxism of European Social Democracy. With its nucleus built around the factory councils and guided by a novel conception of prefigurative struggle (see Chapter 4), *L'Ordine Nuovo* sought to create a *mass* participatory revolutionary movement directly linked to the everyday needs and demands of the working class, situated outside the mediating framework of parties, trade unions, and local government. Its main goal, as Gramsci himself articulated it, was to transform mass consciousness in the context of building new political organs of the socialist state. Isolated by the PSI and the victim of massive police repression after the factory occupations of spring 1920, *L'Ordine Nuovo* disintegrated as rapidly as it appeared. Its theoretical influence lived on, however, to become one of the motivating forces in the founding of the Italian Communist Party the following year. But the PCI, an isolated sect dominated not by the *Ordinovisti* but by the 'abstentionist' faction of Amadeo Bordiga, progressed little beyond the PSI in its sensitivity to the issue of mass consciousness. The Bordigans, though ultra-leftists in their total refusal to participate in bourgeois structures, were ultra-Leninists in their emphasis upon the role of centralized organization as a safeguard of revolutionary identity. Thus, at a time when Mussolini was moving to consolidate the fascist dictatorship, the PCI was primarily concerned with preserving the purity of its theory and organizational identity. Gramsci saw in the sectarianism and intransigence of Bordiga's line nothing but political sterility when tactical wisdom demanded a unified popular force (a 'united front' that would not entangle the PCI in *elite* alliances) which could effectively combat fascism. Bordiga was arrested in 1924, and it was not until the Lyons Party Congress in 1926 that Gramsci's position was adopted by the central committee, but by this time the PCI was on the verge of being forced underground with much of its leadership fleeing into exile. And Gramsci himself was arrested in November 1926.

During his more than ten isolated and agonizing years in prison, Gramsci returned again and again to the problem of consciousness as part of his project of outlining a new revolutionary theory. Hardly a page of the *Prison Notebooks* escapes the spirit of this effort. Gramsci's concern for the everyday aspect of politics, his interest in popular attitudes, beliefs, myths, etc. made incarceration all the more painful. He always read popular novels and journals, no matter how 'unsophisticated' they were, in order to understand the pervasive themes that reflected needs, aspirations, and emotions of the Italian people. But after a time Gramsci found that no type of reading in prison could serve this enlightening purpose so long as he was cut off from people. Already in November 1928 he expressed the following sentiments in a letter to his sister-in-law Tatiana:

> I do a great deal of reading. But I enjoy it much less than I used to. Books and magazines contain generalized notions and only sketch the course of events in the world as best they can; they never let you have an immediate, direct, animated sense of the lives of Tom, Dick and Harry. If you're not able to understand real individuals, you can't understand what is universal and general.[8]

Ironically, Gramsci's own theoretical contributions in the *Prison Notebooks* remain powerful despite the absence of this immediate dialectic between the 'animate' and the 'universal' – but of course Gramsci had plenty to draw on from his pre-prison experiences.

In the prison writings, Gramsci characterized revolutionary process as involving a long series of ideological encounters that take place on a 'higher plane than the economy'; a decisive rupture with the past could never occur without a profound consciousness transformation in the great majority of people. With unassailable logic, he observed that the objective conditions for socialist revolution (i.e. alienation and exploitation in capitalist society) had existed in Europe for several decades, but nowhere had there been a revolution. What had been lacking was the subjective element (mass socialist consciousness) that could impart political meaning to the ongoing crisis of capitalism.

> It may be ruled out that immediate economic crises of themselves produce fundamental historical events; they can simply create a terrain more favourable to the dissemination of certain modes of thought, and certain ways of posing and resolving questions involving the entire subsequent development of national life.[9]

Gramsci actually envisaged a dialectical interplay between structural and ideological elements, but he wanted to focus upon the moment at which collective consciousness becomes active and intervenes to transform structures, making possible the qualitative movement from capitalism to socialism. Consciousness for Gramsci was not an abstract realm of thought, detached from everyday life, but rather a *concrete political force* – a complex combination of ideas, beliefs, feelings, and sentiments that are integral to the experiences of a particular 'collective organism' (a social stratum or class) and are a defining characteristic of political action. Consciousness not only shapes political struggle, but is the medium through which the popular strata emerge as self-determining revolutionary subjects.

The theoretical approach to mass struggle that Gramsci develops in the *Prison Notebooks* has much in common with Rosa Luxemburg's earlier focus upon the problematic of popular consciousness (e.g. in the conception of the 'mass strike' outlined after the Russian Revolution of 1905) and with Georges Sorel's vision of the proletarian myth of the General Strike.[10] At a time when objectivist Marxism held sway, with its fetishism of 'historical forces' and 'structures', these theorists stood virtually alone in affirming that revolutionary action could only evolve out of the shared norms, language, and emotive symbols (such as 'myths') of popular ideological struggle. And yet in riding the crest of the Hegelian wave of the postwar period, Gramsci was in a position to advance well beyond the tentative and incomplete explorations of Luxemburg and Sorel, both philosophically and strategically. Above all, he was able to move beyond their notions that the proletariat itself, through its own spontaneous self-activity, could achieve liberation.

Gramsci pointed out that orthodox Marxism all too often tended to reify concepts like 'class', 'state', 'party', and 'mode of production', losing sight of the individual human actors that made up these larger social units. He contrasted the socio-psychological dynamic of a voluntarist Marxism with the 'external attitude' typical of the mechanistic approach, which in effect transferred political initiative and responsibility from self-conscious human beings to structural entities possessing a kind of collective personality, thus encouraging immobility:

> The individual expects the organism to act, even if he does not do anything himself, and does not reflect that precisely because his attitude is very widespread, the organism is necessarily inoperative. Furthermore, it should be recognized that, since a deterministic and mechanical conception of history is very widespread ... each individual, seeing that despite his non-intervention something still does happen, tends to think that there indeed exists, over and above individuals, a phantasmagorical being, the abstraction of the collective organism, a kind of autonomous divinity, which does not think with any concrete brain but still thinks, etc.[11]

Gramsci concluded that it would be a grave error for revolutionaries to create hierarchical political structures designed to operate 'above' the realm of everyday mass existence, detached from historically-evolved grass-roots organs such as agrarian collectives, co-operatives, peoples' assemblies, workers' councils, and neighbourhood groups. These institutions might not be 'socialist' in any pure sense at any given time, but they could be transformed into more advanced revolutionary forms through the dialectical, organic presence of 'organized elements'; on the other hand, where organization becamea self-contained political instrumentality, with clear-cut boundaries between politics and daily social life, the popular dimension of struggle is lost.[12] Gramsci had nothing but harsh criticism for Marxists who looked with contempt from their intellectual heights upon the spontaneous or 'primitive' stirrings of revolt among oppressed strata – e.g. populism, social banditry, and the myriad expressions of mysticism or 'millenarianism' in the countryside, and urban insurrection, utopian socialism, and cultural revolt in the cities.[13] He stressed that the activities of real men and women in real history to define their own existence, particularly during the initial stages of creating a movement, were inevitably 'impure' and contradictory, and that only a childish form of Marxism could expect all manifestations of revolt, dissent, and opposition against established authority to follow ideologically coherent lines of development from the very outset, without 'external' mediation. The crucial issue for Gramsci was how socialists could most effectively build upon embryonic popular struggles, for he viewed all expressions of anger, despair, and alienation in class society as potentially erosive of ideological hegemony.

In his famous critique of Bukharin's 'Popular Manual' in the *Prison Notebooks*, Gramsci argued that Marxism, if it were ever to achieve the status of a liberating philosophy, would first have to learn how to analyse and transcend common sense. Marxism could no longer afford the luxury of competing with the old 'systematic philosophies' at the level of high culture; it would have to inject itself into the mundane and routine life of the masses. The historical task of theory was to politicize the incoherent and fragmentary ideas of 'common sense', which takes on multiple characteristics in bourgeois society, instead of searching for a pure revolutionary truth that looks like a 'baroque form of Platonic idealism'. Hence:

> Indeed, because by its nature it tends towards being a mass philosophy, the philosophy of praxis can only be conceived in a polemical form and in the form of perpetual struggle. Nonetheless the starting point must always be that common sense which is the spontaneous philosophy of the multitude and which has to be made ideologically coherent.[14]

Socialist revolution therefore would have to be the product of self-conscious workers and other oppressed strata striving to overturn the barriers to emancipation in their daily bourgeois existence. Gramsci's point of departure here is thus not far removed from the subjectivist Marxism of Luxemburg and Lukacs, though some crucial differences will also become apparent.

Luxemburg's theory was rooted in the notion of the proletariat as subject-object of history – an approach that viewed consciousness as emerging organically out of a long series of political struggles against capitalism. She saw each new rising of the working class, each new confrontation with the bourgeoisie, as part of a progressive awakening that would move the proletariat (or 'masses') closer to revolutionary victory. Marxism was not, as Lenin had concluded, something that would have to be inculcated into the workers from outside; rather, 'socialism is simply the historical tendency of the class struggle of the proletariat in capitalist society against the class rule of the bourgeoisie'.[15] Luxemburg placed great faith in the spontaneous energies of the workers, citing the 1905 Russian Revolution as an example of effective mass action that surged ahead of the conservative party bureaucracies. She noted that the Blanquism of past revolutionary leaderships always asserted politics in a way that repressed conscious popular involvement; it could never get beyond the vision of human beings as manipulated objects.[16] It led to a conception of strategy and tactics developed outside the realm of mass struggles. Thus, in the spirit of combating opportunism and revisionism, Lenin set out to build an 'organization kernel' completely separate from its surrounding milieu, with all initiative reserved to a small nucleus of elites. Luxemburg argued that this was the disastrous consequence of an underdeveloped proletarian consciousness in Russia, where centralism could easily prevail over the popular element. Revolution for the Bolsheviks was perceived as an *event* rather than as *process*, as the tactic of the 'first blow' rather than a long period of consciousness transformation. For Luxemburg, the idea of substituting centralized organization and leadership for creative mass consciousness was a Jacobin fallacy that in the end denied the authenticity of socialism as a subjective revolutionary force.

Luxemburg was really the first theorist to raise these issues within a framework that transcended a naïve anarchistic spontaneism. Her sophisticated analysis of capitalist development, her powerful attack on anarchism, and her scattered positive references to the role of a revolutionary party, workers' councils, and soviets is enough to show that her 'spontaneism' must be qualified. Nonetheless, her theory in the end failed to overcome some of the most debilitating assumptions of the classical Marxism paradigm: a boundless revolutionary faith in the proletariat, a vision of progress within a unilinear conception of historical development, and a tendency to construct strategy around the ultimate crisis and breakdown of capitalism. In this sense Rosa Luxemburg was a spontaneist – a mood that appeared perhaps most clearly in her bitter critique of the Bolshevik Revolution and the Leninist conception of the party. She saw in the logic of capitalist development a process of consciousness transformation that would propel the masses towards socialism, with economic crises serving as a catalyst. 'Revolution' is not something that can be propagated by elites and cadres, but emerges organically out of the anti-capitalist struggles of the workers themselves. This makes more intelligible Luxemburg's vague and unsystematic discussion of the mass party and her failure to explore the role of the councils. In the last instance she is simply thrown back to the masses themselves, with their properties of innate rationality and free self-determination. But such a prospect became increasingly less defensible by the mid-1920s, when the consolidation of capitalism and the rise of fascism raised the whole issue of mass consciousness in a new light.

Lukacs's Marxism was grounded in more elaborate philosophical reasoning than Luxemburg's, but it arrived at many of the same strategic conclusions. In *History and Class Consciousness* we find a monumental effort to restore the role of proletarian subjectivity and consciousness to the revolutionary process. For Lukacs, it was the exploited position of the working class within the capitalist mode of production that set it in opposition to the total system and determined its revolutionary role in history. Socialism thus became not a theory articulated by philosophers and intellectuals but the culmination of the self-activating struggle for survival by a proletariat whose very existence calls into question the logic and priorities of capitalism. The proletariat develops the capacity to liberate itself as it gains a maturity and critical awareness of its class situation, with the extension of bourgeois society to every realm of social activity; the worker 'is driven by the absolutely imperious dictates of his misery – the practical expression of this necessity – . . . to rebel against this inhumanity'.[17] It followed from this that in Lukacs's perspective there could be no external criteria for evaluating consciousness independent of the imputed historical definition of the proletariat itself; nor could there be political thinking outside the everyday life of the working class that was not in some way bourgeois. There could be no 'state of the future' independent of the proletarian movement itself, which 'is the conscious subject of total social reality'.[18] In his penetrating critique of what passed for orthodox Marxism, Lukacs rejected the assumption of a pure theory outside the development of the class struggle itself, and he challenged any presumed 'scientific' understanding of history independent of human consciousness. Like Luxemburg, he viewed the proletariat as the subject-object of revolutionary transformation, but he emphasized the role of crisis and cataclysmic upheaval much less than she did.

Since Lukacs defined the working class as the universal revolutionary subject by virtue of its antagonistic position vis-à-vis the bourgeoisie, he was never really able to come to grips with the historically specific manifestations of popular consciousness and the concrete tasks of penetrating bourgeois ideological hegemony (or 'reification' in Lukacs's terms). Divorced from its variable and contradictory psychological components, class consciousness in Lukacs's framework became little more than the assigned world-historical mission of the proletariat, a kind of designated consciousness that implied the same kind of optimistic faith in revolutionary progress that was expressed in Luxemburg's Marxism. The premise that the working class through its own self-activity would spontaneously realize socialist consciousness has been overturned many times since the initial appearance of *History and Class Consciousness*; no better proof of Lukacs's inability to ground a political strategy in his particular version of spontaneism is to be found than in his own reversion to Leninism when he took up the question of organization. The theoretical failure here, as Andrew Arato has suggested, resulted from the anticipation of a specific set of attributes of class consciousness at the beginning instead of viewing them as an open-ended, problematical (and thus *constructed*) phenomenon.[19]

Gramsci shared the Luxemburg-Lukacs disenchantment with mechanistic Marxism as well as their commitment to spell out an alternative theory grounded in an understanding of mass consciousness, but he was more sensitive to the pitfalls of spontaneism than were either Luxemburg or Lukacs. The fact is that he started out by completely accepting Lenin's critique of spontaneity initially formulated in *What is to be Done?*, which supplied much of the strategic thinking behind the development of the Bolshevik Party. Lenin viewed working-class consciousness in its 'given' form as essentially the reproduction of bourgeois values and life-styles rather than their negation; the kinds of innovative leadership, theoretical comprehension, and vision of the future required to transform capitalism and construct a socialist society were not likely to develop organically out of proletarian everyday life itself because the practical survival mentality of the oppressed could never lead to anything beyond a preoccupation with concrete immediacies. Lenin attacked the spontaneists (who were also 'economists') in Russia for restricting the labour movement to its lowest stage in development in their equation of 'socialism' with the 'proletariat' independent of the specific content of its thought and action. While the workers would normally be aware of the need for a change in their life-situation, such awareness could not be expected to lead automatically to a revolutionary belief system but would more probably, as history had shown, result in a reformism seeking partial objectives within the dominant order. Lenin concluded that only the intervention of an 'external' *political* force could reverse the omnipresent trend towards reformism and opportunism. Only a centralized organization composed of full-time professional cadres could mobilize the popular strata around socialist goals and preserve revolutionary identity in a largely antagonistic milieu. In the actual historical development of Leninism through the Russian Revolution of 1917 and the period of the civil war, centralist tendencies within the party were so intensified that any political stirring outside the Bolshevik party structure itself came to be defined as 'petty bourgeois' or even 'counter-revolutionary'. Such spontaneous elements (including even the workers' councils and soviets) were eventually either subordinated to the party or eliminated altogether. In the end, organization and leadership were the primary vehicles of revolutionary transformation for Lenin, the repositories of Marxist theory and strategy; socialist consciousness was an *elite* phenomenon that, at best, could only be injected into mass struggles from outside.

Gramsci stands somewhere between the spontaneist leanings of Luxemburg and Lukacs and the Jacobin centralism of Lenin.[20] The latter's conviction that revolutionary change would depend upon the insertion of an 'external element' into the class struggle had influenced Gramsci, especially after the failure of the *Ordine Nuovo* movement in 1921, when he began to look for a more explicitly political solution to the Marxist revolutionary project;[21] it is his increasing preoccupation with this 'external element' (the role of the intellectuals, the function of the party) that informs Gramsci's writing in the *Prison Notebooks*. In other words, Gramsci sought to refine and expand Lenin's approach to the problem of mass consciousness. What was needed was a conceptual framework that could provide an *historical* understanding of the different expressions that anti-capitalist opposition might assume. Given his theory of ideological hegemony, Gramsci concluded that spontaneous, unmediated revolt was always contained by the pre-existing categories of thought and behaviour and that it was precisely in *transcending* the concreteness of its position in capitalist society that the proletariat could move towards a revolutionary definition of its self-activity. How such transcendence might be realized was the starting point of theoretical investigation, the uppermost concern of Marxists who could no longer deny the existence of *diverse* tendencies (including fascist ones) within the working class itself, and not some presupposition based upon the role of 'natural' forces in history. Socialism could no longer be viewed as the organic outgrowth of a maturing proletariat in advanced capitalism but as a set of objectives to be won in the process of creative political construction, or architectonics. What had been lacking in Luxemburg and Lukacs, despite their ground-breaking attempts to overcome the inertia of mechanistic Marxism, was a concretely positive, transformative element that could give shape to revolutionary strategy.[22]

For Gramsci, the central dilemma was how to move the oppressed beyond the immediacy of their everyday concerns without at the same time obliterating their spontaneous energies. It would be the function of revolutionary theory to impart a sense of identity to political struggles and to expand the challenge to every restricting influence of the established order, including the forms of popular consciousness generally referred to as 'common sense'. Whereas the anarchists and spontaneists had tended to glorify common sense as innately progressive, Gramsci viewed it as a disaggregated collection of sentiments, ideals, myths, superstitions, etc. in which 'one can find there anything one likes',[23] whether conservative or reformist, reactionary or revolutionary. As he put it in one of his final pre-prison articles:

There exists in the totality of the working masses many distinct wills: there is a communist will, a maximalist will, a reformist will, a liberal democratic will. There is even a fascist will, in a certain sense and within certain limits. So long as there exists a bourgeois regime, with a monopoly of the press in the hands of capitalism and thus the possibility of the government and political parties to impose political issues according to their interests, presented as the general interest, so long as the freedom of association and meetings of the working class are suppressed and restricted, so long as the most impudent lies against communism are diffused at will, it is inevitable that the working class will remain fragmented, that is with many different wills.[24]

This idea of a contradictory and ambiguous mass consciousness is one that Gramsci adhered to throughout the *Prison Notebooks*. The potential for socialist consciousness would therefore ultimately depend upon a critique and transcendence of 'natural' or narrowly-pragmatic belief systems insofar as 'common sense is an ambiguous, contradictory, and multiform concept, and that to refer to common sense as a confirmation of truth is nonsense'.[25] Gramsci went on to point out that Catholicism was precisely the kind of ideology that indulged the masses in their fragmentary and superstitious attitudes, in their spontaneity, whereas it should be the role of Marxism as a *popular Weltanschauung* to raise mass consciousness above this mundane level – to create 'good sense' in place of 'common sense' (*senso buono* as opposed to *senso comune*). Because of the pervasiveness of ideological hegemony, all 'immediate' or unmediated responses would inevitably be conditioned by dominant structures and values; common sense, therefore, could never be more than a negation – and a distorted negation at that – of the old order. It could not bear positive elements of the new.[26]

One of the consistent themes of Gramsci's thought was the proposition that critical awareness emerges neither strictly out of the social reality of productive relations nor out of a cataclysmic 'explosion'. It is this which sets him apart from all previous Marxist conceptions, including even Leninism to the extent that it, too, relied heavily upon the moment of crisis. Gramsci defined revolutionary consciousness as both a moral-intellectual and political phenomenon, evolving initially outside the organic processes of everyday struggle among the oppressed strata. Thus:

> Ideas and opinions are not spontaneously 'born' in each individual brain: they have had a centre of formation, of irradiation, of dissemination, of persuasion – a group of men, or a single individual even, which has developed them and presented them in the current form of political reality.[27]

Though all social groups possess at least an embryonic world-view, with its distorted and incoherent image of reality, their 'common sense' is never fixed and stable but is constantly changing through the influence of new philosophical and scientific discoveries. It takes on a revolutionary political content only with the introduction of a powerful counter-hegemonic force (the 'external element') that is capable of diffusing an alternative socialist world-view. Without such a force, popular revolt is destined to be absorbed by the prevailing hegemony or perhaps even channelled in the direction of reactionary populism. Gramsci had in mind the ideological inroads into the working class and peasantry made by fascism in Italy when he noted that 'neglecting, or worse still despising, so-called spontaneous movements, i.e. failing to give them a conscious leadership or to raise them to a higher plane by inserting them into politics may often have extremely serious consequences'.[28]

Revolutionary mass consciousness – the internalization of broad socialist beliefs and values among the 'rising' groups – never simply 'appears', according to Gramsci, but evolves as part of an historical transformation in which the external forces (e.g. Marxist intellectuals of bourgeois origins) play a 'leading' role in demystifying ideological hegemony and in opening up new ways of understanding the alienation of class society. The expression that workers and peasants initially give to their discontent is generally diffuse and fragmentary, and it often moves into a simple anti-authoritarianism such as 'dislike of officialdom – the only form in which the state is perceived'. Gramsci observed that 'this "generic" hatred is still "semi-feudal" rather than modern in character, and cannot be taken as evidence of class consciousness – merely as the first glimmer of such consciousness, in other words, merely as the basic negative, polemical attitude'.[29] At any given moment, therefore, mass opposition may give rise to partial, confused ideologies or 'utopias' that might constitute the basis of a more mature critical consciousness (Marxism), again depending upon the intervention of political leadership. There was also the possibility that it would drift back into a sense of fatalistic despair and passivity in the wake of repression or serious political failures; the mood of the rural masses in the Italian *Mezzogiorno* (the South and Sicily), which Gramsci had studied very closely, typically swung back and forth between the two poles of passivity and spontaneous revolt.

The crucial problem here was how to transcend the parochial concreteness of spontaneous consciousness – how, in other words, to move from the objective reality of oppression to revolutionary subjectivity. For Gramsci, this transition entailed a fundamental change in popular consciousness: from the 'corporate-economic' to the political, where the question of the *state*, or total society is raised to the point at which the interests of one group 'can and must become the interests of other subordinate groups too'. It is this equation of the political with mature socialist consciousness that is central to Gramsci's Marxism, a point we shall elaborate further in Chapter 5 below. The 'corporate' stage of consciousness, rooted in a narrow sense of economic self-interest (for example much of the trade union movement), could never pass beyond bourgeois reformism; its assertion of specific claims within limited sectors of the economy (crafts, occupations, enterprises) denied the possibility of class solidarity, not to mention the building of multi-class alliances. To reach a political understanding of anti-capitalist struggle meant to oppose the very totality of the bourgeois system, including the entire foundations of legitimacy upon which class domination rests. As Gramsci put it:

> This is the most purely political phase, and marks the decisive passage from the structure to the sphere of complex superstructures; it is the phase in which previously germinated ideologies become 'party,' come into confrontation and conflict, until only one of them, or at least a single combination of them, tends to prevail, to gain the upper hand, to propagate not only a unison of economic and political aims, but also

intellectual and moral unity, posing all the questions around which the struggle rages not on a corporate but on a 'universal' plane, and thus creating the hegemony of a fundamental social group over a series of subordinate groups.[30]

While the initial catalyst of this consciousness transformation may come from the stratum of revolutionary intellectuals — a mediating force outside the production process itself — Gramsci argued that the masses themselves must become in the long run the bearer of revolutionary change. It is they, rather than an organized party leadership, who must ultimately create socialism; otherwise, political struggle only serves to reproduce the hierarchical social and authority relations of bourgeois society. The new consciousness, if it is to provide the basis of an 'integrated culture' of its own, must be embodied in everyday social processes instead of remaining the preserve of party elites. Moreover, while revolution involves an intellectual-ideological dimension as well as an institutional one, theory and strategy can only be advanced as part of concrete human existence in its totality, never as an autonomous struggle restricted to the intellectuals. Gramsci wrote that 'the principle must always rule that ideas are not born of other ideas, philosophies of other philosophies; they are a continually renewed expression of real historical development'.[31] Again, the dialectical quality of Gramsci's Marxism stands out clearly through his attempt to overcome the polar dualism of intellectual *vs.* popular, organization and leadership *vs.* the spontaneous, and theoretical *vs.* everyday life. This is one of the characteristics of the *Prison Notebooks* that makes Gramsci's thought unique, that enables him to incorporate into his theory the positive contributions of Luxemburg, Lukacs, and Lenin alike. In reflecting upon his own previous role in the *Ordine Nuovo* movement of the early postwar years, Gramsci summed up his approach to consciousness in the following way:

> It [the leadership] applied itself to real men, formed in specific historical relations, with specific feelings, outlooks, fragmentary conceptions of the world, etc. . . . This element of 'spontaneity' was not neglected and even less despised. It was educated, directed, purged of extraneous contaminations; the aim was to bring it into line with modern theory [i.e. Marxism] — but in a living and historically effective

manner. The leaders themselves spoke of the 'spontaneity' of the movement, and rightly so. This assertion was a stimulus, a tonic, an element of unification in depth . . . It gave the masses a 'theoretical' consciousness of being creators of historical and institutional values, of being founders of a state. This unity between 'spontaneity' and 'conscious leadership' or 'discipline' is precisely the real political action of the subaltern classes, insofar as this is mass politics and not merely an adventure by groups claiming to represent the masses.[32]

The theoretical synthesis that Gramsci began to elaborate here took account of the limitations of Leninism and classical Marxism alike in its organic linkage of the revolutionary intellectual world-view and the mass belief system within the same totality. Theory and consciousness are thus integrated through the medium of popular revolutionary struggle; intellectuals and masses are shaped by the same historical and ideological processes, and must therefore struggle against the fetters of hegemony in unison. While the intellectual stratum articulates a new conception of the world by guiding, teaching and inspiring, it does not – in the strict Leninist sense – become the final repository of revolutionary ideas or the vehicle for constructing socialism. Historical subjectivity belongs to the workers and allied groupings who must comprehend the new potential in their daily thought and action, i.e. to the 'collective man' who becomes transformed in the process of transforming bourgeois society. This is why Gramsci sometimes metaphorically referred to socialist revolution as the 'modern popular Reformation'. He viewed Marxism not as an abstract philosophy but as a material force that encompasses the whole complex of human existence, the '*ensemble* of social relations' that brings together economics, politics, culture, and social life. To perpetuate the mechanical divorce between elite theory and mass consciousness would only deny the creative democratic energies needed to construct a permanent cultural revolution.

His emphasis upon ideological hegemony, consciousness, and totality led Gramsci to devote considerable attention to the role of intellectuals. The term 'intellectual' did not connote for Gramsci a particular kind of individual but rather a universal function – a set of activities, broadly 'moral' in content, that serve to either undermine or advance various world-views. All human communication could therefore be seen as intellectual in nature because

> Each man, finally, outside his professional activity, carries on some form of intellectual activity, that is, he is a 'philosopher', an artist, a man of taste, he participates in a particular conception of the world, has a conscious line of moral conduct, and therefore contributes to sustain a conception of the world or to modify it, that is, to bring into being new modes of thought.[33]

Gramsci had in mind a wide range of activities – e.g. culture, social relations, life-styles, education – that could be called 'intellectual' to the extent they affected one way or another the ongoing 'war of position'. The intellectual realm, therefore, was not conceived of as a specialized set of mental functions, confined to a narrow elite, but as an integral part of political struggle grounded in everyday life. Thus:

> The mode of being of the new intellectual can no longer consist in eloquence, which is an exterior and momentary mover of feelings and passions, but in active participation in practical life, as constructor, organizer, 'permanent persuader', and not just a simple orator . . .[34]

To be effective, intellectuals must be an organic part of a community; they must articulate new values within the shared language and symbols of the larger culture.

But Gramsci also realized that not all people are intellectuals in the same way at any given historical moment; socialist consciousness embraces an identifiable system of values that sets it apart from common sense and the various hegemonic ideologies, and it develops unevenly within bourgeois society as a whole. Socialist intellectuals thus perform functions that are in some sense more 'advanced' – functions that are diffuse in the early stages but which, through the gradual expansion of mass struggles, tend to cohere within the broad activities of education and cultural transformation. One concrete embodiment of the intellectual function, though by no means the only one, is the revolutionary party, which Gramsci often referred to as the 'collective intellectual' or 'myth prince' to distinguish it from a centralized vanguard elite. The party was for Gramsci the repository less of 'scientific truth' than a 'moral-intellectual' world-view that could provide the basis of an ideologically homogeneous movement. Marxism would never gain ascendancy simply because of the logical consistency of its analysis or the 'knowledge' it could supply, nor because of the theoretical contributions of great thinkers, important as these might be. On the contrary: 'The most important element is undoubtedly one whose character is determined not by reason but by faith.'[35] 'Philosophy' and 'theory' become vital only where they culminate in norms of collective action, at which point the level of popular consciousness is transformed to such an extent that the separation between intellectuals and masses is transcended and everyone becomes an intellectual in the full, liberated (Marxist) sense.

During the long struggle for ideological hegemony, the revolutionary intellectuals would have to take the initiative on many fronts: raising new questions and introducing new modes of thinking about reality, attacking the accepted wisdom of established intellectual authorities, and providing theoretical guidance to emerging mass struggles. In bourgeois society, however, given the prevailing definition of intellectuals as either scientific-technical 'experts' or 'learned men of culture', this form of ideological combat always threatens to become elitist and even obscurantist, since even Marxists tend to fall prey to traditional paradigms of intellectual discourse. The capitalist social division of labour perpetuates the separation between mental and physical work; intellectual life encourages highly-specialized modes of thinking that are carried on in a language remote from and unintelligible to the general populace. This has increasingly reinforced one of the classical dilemmas of Marxist movements: a vicious circle of elitism and political isolation on the part of intellectuals and anti-intellectualism (and thus also anti-Marxism) among the lower classes.

Gramsci's way out of this dilemma was the formation of groupings of 'organic' intellectuals that would be both 'leading' and 'representative' in the crucial respect of being part of the everyday social existence of the working class. New ideas would not be introduced or 'propagandized' as extraneous inputs into mass politics but would be integrated into the very fabric of proletarian culture, life-styles, language, traditions, etc. by revolutionaries who themselves worked and lived within the same environment. Only this could ensure the dialectical relationship between theory and practice, the intellectual and the spontaneous, the political and the social, which could lay the foundations of an authentic *Marxist* subjectivity in popular consciousness itself. Intellectual defectors from the bourgeoisie would have an initial role to play — a factor that Kautsky had earlier exaggerated — but long-range revolutionary transformation would have to depend upon the function of the 'organic' intellectuals. Hence:

> One of the most important characteristics of any group that is developing towards dominance is its struggle to assimilate and conquer 'ideologically' the traditional intellectuals, but this assimilation and conquest is made quicker and more efficacious the more the group in question succeeds in simultaneously elaborating its own intellectuals.[36]

This 'internal' principle (what might be called the 'internalization of the external element') was more than Gramsci's attempt to escape the Jacobin authoritarianism inherent in Lenin's model of revolution; it was also an effort to create a more *effective* strategy by grounding it in a continuous historical process.[37]

The concept of the 'organic' intellectual supplied the vital linkage in Gramsci's theory between the intellectual sphere (where Marxism had originated) and popular consciousness; it not only imparted to his thought a depth that was lacking in both the Second and Third Internationals but also laid the foundations of a *total* conception of revolution — merging the poles of thought and action, universal and particular, cognitive and emotive. It was through the mediating role of the 'organic' intellectuals that Marxism, as the first truly popular *Weltanschauung* in history, would emerge as a real counter-hegemonic force. 'From the disintegration of Hegelianism derives the beginning of a new cultural process, different in character from its predecessors, a process in which practical movement and theoretical thought are united,' Gramsci wrote, adding that '. . . a new way of conceiving the world and man is born and that this conception is no longer reserved to the great intellectuals, to professional philosophers, but tends to become a popular, "mass" phenomenon . . .'.[38] But for this to happen, Marxism would have to permanently combat the old contradictions of social life as they are expressed throughout bourgeois society:

> The popular element 'feels' but does not always know or understand; the intellectual element 'knows' but does not always understand and in particular does not always feel. The two extremes are therefore pedantry and philistinism on the one hand and blind passion on the other . . . The intellectual's error consists in believing that one can know without understanding and even more without feeling and being impassioned: in other words that the intellectual can be an intellectual if distinct and separate from the people-nation, i.e. without feeling the elementary passions of the people . . . One cannot make politics-history without this passion, without this sentimental connection between intellectuals and people-nation.[39]

Another problem stemmed from the task of integrating Marxist theory into the everyday existence of the working class (or 'people-nation') without simultaneously compromising the revolutionary identity of the movement or the objectives of socialism. Gramsci was keenly aware of the way in which previous world-views (e.g. the Reformation, late Christianity, Social Democracy) had degenerated as they strived to reach outward, incorporating in the process many diverse and contradictory popular elements. The dilemma revealed itself historically as one of isolation *vs.* compromise, sectarianism *vs.* incorporation. With the collapse of the parties of the Second International, the problem of political identity came to the forefront of socialist theorizing: how would it be possible to retain revolutionary consciousness in a contaminating bourgeois environment, where every institution serves to perpetuate hegemony? Lenin's solution was centralized organization, Sorel's was ideological passion or 'myth', and Luxemburg's was the energy of masses themselves. Gramsci's solution combined all of these, with the 'organic' intellectuals emerging as the repository of revolutionary values.

Yet, since Gramsci stressed that socialism could never be imposed from above but would have to be the self-conscious expression of the oppressed groups themselves, it was clear that identity would have to be risked in the process of transforming mass consciousness, which entailed democratic participation in all areas of social and political life; Gramsci's rejection of Bordiga's purist abstentionism in the early years of the PCI originated from this perspective. So too did his distrust of all elite politics, whether in the form of a centralized party or frontist-type alliances from above — a theme that permeates not only the *Prison Notebooks* but is consistent from the early factory council days to his 'united front' strategy and the PCI programme he helped to formulate at the Lyons Congress in 1926. Leadership and theoretical direction would ultimately have to merge with the self-activity of the masses, working through structures of their own creation (e.g. the councils).

Whereas from Gramsci's viewpoint ultra-Leninist organization, in its effort to combat political degeneration, actually stifled mass initiative, alliances and coalitions with bourgeois parties only shifted the focus away from the permanent task of generating a counter-hegemonic movement. Although Gramsci was in prison and nearing the end of his life in the mid-thirties when the Comintern implemented the Popular Front tactics of building anti-fascist coalitions within bourgeois structures, there is evidence that he had earlier opposed PCI adoption of a similar policy.[40] In any case, he surely would have recoiled at the way in which this version of frontism became institutionalized as a general strategy for the post-Second World War PCI, whose leadership has ironically chosen to invoke the stature of Gramsci as 'founding father' to legitimate this very strategy — a strategy that has led to the kind of political degeneration Gramsci himself would have predicted. The PCI failed to maintain its revolutionary identity precisely because it operated *exclusively* within parliament, trade unions, local administrations, etc. thus gradually adopting the logic of bourgeois social and authority relations, instead of attempting to create *alternative popular* forms of socialist democracy along the lines suggested by Gramsci.[41]

One of the main theoretical extensions of Gramsci's approach to consciousness was his conception of a unified 'bloc' of diverse social forces that evolves outside the established parliamentary and trade union structures. Gramsci employed the terms 'ideological bloc', 'political bloc', and 'historical bloc' to refer to an historically-congealed synthesis of popular movements – a homogeneous grouping defined not in terms of objective sociological categories but according to its concrete political expression. By 'bloc' Gramsci therefore meant considerably more than simple alliances, coalitions, or loose configurations of political groups; what he envisaged was an amalgamation of forces, always shifting and changing, that emerges at a specific historical conjuncture. It was a construct that linked history and politics, structure and superstructure within an 'ensemble of ideas and social relations', interests and political action, leading to a process whereby 'popular feelings became unified' and gave form to struggle.[42] In the *Prison Notebooks* Gramsci discussed a wide range of possibilities, such as 'national blocs', 'urban blocs', and 'Southern rural blocs', in which different social groups come together as homogeneous *movements* through a shared ideological bond.

This very important strategic conception draws attention to the complex cultural and ideological processes taking place in everyday life within civil society. It suggests the building of popular alliances that transcend an exclusive class basis and coalesce around psychological-emotive forces at work during a given historical moment, such as nationalism, anti-clericalism, regional separatism, and ethnic identity. Though anti-socialist in most cases, these appeals might function as broad radicalizing catalysts in times of crisis or ferment, linking up previously antagonistic strata (e.g. workers and peasants) in a counter-hegemonic movement. Gramsci argued that political struggle could not be viewed as a 'pure' manifestation of class conflict between proletariat and bourgeoisie, but would have to be understood as a mediated process based upon a particular constellation of issues, priorities, and ideological preferences having no strict relation to material conditions. He rejected as metaphysics the assumption that particular classes and groups are the historical carriers of a singular revolutionary consciousness, since it ignored the crucial variations of mediating factors *within* classes and from country to country. The creation of durable solidary 'blocs' – not temporary alliances or elite coalitions – was for Gramsci a primary strategic task, one that was motivated by a number of strategic insights: the value of mass ideological solidarity, the role of nationalism and the uniqueness of the Italian situation, the tendency towards diversification of the proletariat in advanced capitalism, and the imperatives of linking the anti-capitalist struggles of Northern Italian workers with the anti-feudal struggles of peasants in the *Mezzogiorno*.[43]

All of this is consistent with Gramsci's advocacy of a 'united front' strategy for the PCI in the early twenties, through which it would be possible to unite workers, peasants, and petty bourgeoisie in a *popular alliance* opposed to the leadership of established parties and unions. With the emergence of fascism he began to support more vigorously a policy of mass mobilization (for example, extension of the factory and peasants' committees) that could simultaneously counter the Mussolini regime *and* preserve the goals of socialism, which Gramsci still believed to be on the agenda. The Popular Front line adopted later by the Comintern was the direct antithesis of this revolutionary strategy, since the former defended while the latter attacked bourgeois institutions and political groups. Gramsci's conception was that of discrediting party elites (including the 'semi-fascist' leadership of the PSI itself) as a means of elevating mass consciousness and attracting popular support for the PCI. Before Gramsci's arrest in 1926, the PCI had in fact begun to push the idea of workers' and peasants' committees in both North and South as a means of expanding its own limited membership (about 30,000) and mass base, although by then it was already too late. The Lyons Theses, in great measure authored by Gramsci, stressed the long-range construction of a homogeneous bloc of 'national-popular' forces composed primarily of peasants and workers, organized from below in opposition to the reformist union and party bureaucracies. Gramsci thus found himself situated between the abstentionist and isolationist 'left' position taken earlier by Bordiga and later by the Sixth Comintern Congress (1928), and the Popular Front approach of participating within and defending bourgeois institutions in the struggle against fascism. Despite the weakness of Gramsci's analysis of the fascist phenomenon in Italy, one is struck by the continuity of his strategic ideas from the early twenties to his formulations in the *Prison Notebooks*.

Though Gramsci's original contributions to a Marxist understanding of mass consciousness were fragmentary and incomplete, he did succeed in theoretically integrating the role of ideas and consciousness into a total conception of revolutionary transformation. Grounded in the notion of ideological hegemony, his strategic vision liberated the intellectual and psychological dimension of socialist politics that had been repressed for so long within the Second International. Gramsci broadened the scope and meaning of revolution to the extent that it transcended simultaneously the limited perspectives of the classical Marxists, the spontaneists, and the Jacobins. As opposed to the orthodox theorists, Gramsci took consciousness to be a problem rather than a given, and moved from there to renounce ahistorical, vulgar materialism and affirm the indispensable role of revolutionary subjectivity. As opposed to the spontaneists, he never accepted the faith that a mature revolutionary movement could emerge organically out of the self-activity of the oppressed classes, or that the proletariat would unveil its universality and move towards socialism in much the same way the bourgeoisie rose to destroy feudalism. The workers, in this sense, could never be viewed as the creators of a new mode of production from their position within capitalism itself; what was needed to make the leap was a coherent intellectual grasp of history and the role of particular groups in it, a well-developed strategy, and new forms of popular organization.

Finally, as opposed to the ultra-centralist Jacobins within the Marxist tradition, Gramsci went beyond the notion of consciousness as primarily an 'external' or elite phenomenon – the preserve of a party vanguard that places itself 'above' the masses organizationally and politically and distrusts any manifestation of spontaneity. In contrast to the strict Leninist model, with its elitist and authoritarian direction, Gramsci sought an organic fusion of the external and internal, theoretical and spontaneous, elite and popular elements of political struggle. The difference between Lenin and Gramsci, often obscured by Gramsci's great respect for Lenin, was that in the final analysis Gramsci saw the revolutionary process as a *total* and *popular* (or 'national-popular') phenomenon; whereas the external moving force of theory-intellectuals-party must always be present, it is not a superimposed but an *internalized* force, with the oppressed groups of the 'revolutionary historical bloc' pressing their claims as political subjects in the momentous struggle to assert a new socialist hegemony.

4. The Factory Councils: Nucleus of the 'New State'

For all of his emphasis upon the role of ideological struggle in the revolutionary process, Gramsci never at any point ignored the vital question of what kinds of structures should give institutional expression to the new 'integrated culture' of socialism. Much more than the other theoretical and political currents within the European left – anarchism, syndicalism, Social Democracy, and Leninism – Gramscian strategy advanced a dialectical conception of the relationship between consciousness and structures, between the general development of socialist revolution and its immediate, localized realization. This is reflected most clearly in the *Ordine Nuovo* writings of 1919–1922, when the imminent concerns of revolution were uppermost in Gramsci's mind, but it also carries over into his PCI contributions of 1921–1926 and to a lesser extent into the *Prison Notebooks* themselves, as the urgency of political involvement begins to decline. The general perspective that emerges from Gramsci's theoretical work is a structural dualism combining the factory councils, soviets, and other organs of popular socialist democracy with the revolutionary party as a mechanism of co-ordination and leadership. It was his systematic integration of the council movement into the Marxist tradition, rooted in the innovative and heroic practice of the Turin proletariat itself, that lent concreteness to Gramsci's unique strategy – to his notion of counter-hegemonic struggle, to his critique of bourgeois party and union structures and of the elitist authoritarianism implicit in the concept 'dictatorship of the proletariat'. Through his understanding of the councils as the prefiguration of the new order within bourgeois society, Gramsci raised the attack upon bureaucracy to a more positive level than that reached by the anarchists, Rosa Luxemburg, Michels, or even the later versions of 'council Communism'.

On the surface, Gramsci's approach would not seem to be a great departure from original Bolshevik strategy, which had also encouraged the development of workers' councils and soviets as structures of 'dual power' in Russia during the revolutionary ferment of 1917. Indeed, many of the *Ordinovisti* theories were borrowed from the Russian context in the early post-revolutionary period. But the reality of political developments after the October Revolution, accelerated not only by the failure of European revolutionary prospects but by Lenin's highly-centralized conception of the party, soon contradicted all expectations of self-management and democractic participation.

Though Gramsci's early writings contain little that is explicitly critical of either Lenin or tendencies in Soviet development, his articles and essays in *L'Ordine Nuovo* reveal a highly-sensitive awareness of these general problems. There were two dimensions to the issue of structures. On the one hand, the dominant institutions – parliament, state bureaucracy, parties, trade unions, etc. – originated within bourgeois society and could only function within its logic; though important as a *tactical* means of reaching the masses, these structures were *strategically* very limited if not in fact co-optative, and hence would have to be transcended in the form of prefigurative bodies such as the councils. On the other hand, while Gramsci saw in a revolutionary party the necessary political mechanism for coordinating diverse struggles and taking up the 'war of movement' (the actual assault on state power), he also argued strongly for the councils and other 'dual power' structures as counter-weights to the Bonapartist tendencies inherent in any centralized organization. Here Gramsci insisted that it would be necessary to build '*new forms* of state life' that could organically transform social and authority relations as part of the 'war of position', rather than produce another 'government by functionaries'. The appearance of such popular institutions would minimize the dangers of reproducing hegemonic ideologies and social relations under a new political banner, to the extent that they would embrace or at least anticipate the socialist principles of the future 'collective society'.[1]

Gramsci's insightful early critiques of the trade union and party structures that claimed to represent the Italian working class movement provided the springboard for his theory of the councils. Since both the unions and parties were born on the terrain of liberal democracy, Gramsci reasoned, they could never transcend the logic of capitalism itself; each was a phenomenon of the bourgeois stage of development, with its narrow, framented definition of economics and politics. Hence to seek anti-capitalist, revolutionary objectives within that arena could only serve to perpetuate the illusion that liberation is possible under capitalism, or that 'victories' within bourgeois society were somehow a first step in the direction of socialism. Gramsci argued that, quite to the contrary, the strategic utilization of liberal institutions by Marxist movements was intrinsically contradictory – the inevitable result of which was the integration of the proletariat into the capitalist order. The comfortable inclination to operate through a 'given' structural framework only helped to stifle the development of revolutionary consciousness by downgrading implicitly the need to create new mass-based socialist organs of economic production and political authority.

The trade unions, from Gramsci's point of view, increasingly constituted a central element of bourgeois hegemony. In the first place, they articulated a notion of labour as a commodity to be bought, sold, and negotiated within the corporate structure, and consequently advanced only the limited economic demands of a particular sector. Most unions defined workers as consumers rather than *producers* who themselves had created the material foundations of the capitalist economy and who therefore could play a major role in transforming it. Secondly, Gramsci saw trade unions as an expression of capitalist legality insofar as they sought to establish a contractual relationship between wage labour and industrial management within the shared norms of the corporate economy. In this sense, they were 'objectively nothing other than a commercial society, of a clearly capitalist type, that attempts to realize on behalf of the proletariat the maximum price for wage labour . . .'[2] They were not committed to overturning bourgeois legality itself nor were they anxious to challengé the very nature of wage labour as an aspect of capitalist exploitation. Thirdly, as the unions expanded in scope and membership they became, like all other corporate structures, increasingly bureaucratic and remote from the needs of the great mass of workers; they could assert economic demands but could never raise the more challenging issue of self-management or *workers' control*, since this would threaten the vested interests of union leadership. Over time, the union hierarchy became as fearful and even contemptuous of mass *political* struggles as the bourgeoisie:

> ... the union bureaucrat conceives industrial legality as a permanent state of affairs. He too often defends it from the same viewpoint as the proprietor. He sees only chaos and wilfullness in everything that emerges from the working masses. He does not understand the workers' rebellion ...[3]

Gramsci concluded from his analysis of the Marxist-dominated CGIL (Italian General Confederation of Labour) and other Italian union organizations that, while the trade union movement might secure significant economic gains for large sectors of the working class, it had become such an institutionalized fixture of capitalist society that it could not really contribute to any broadly-defined socialist revolution. Its narrow reformist focus and bureaucratized structure perpetuated in the proletariat precisely the kind of reified consciousness that had bound it to the bourgeois order. In other words, far from instilling revolutionary consciousness, the unions functioned to reproduce capitalist hegemony:

> The essential nature of the union is competitive, not communist. The union cannot be the instrument for a radical transformation of society; it can provide the proletariat with proficient bureaucrats, technical experts on industrial questions of a general sort, but it cannot be the basis of proletarian power. It offers no possibility of fostering the individual abilities of proletarians which make them capable and worthy of governing society; it cannot produce the leadership that will embody the vital forces and rhythm of the development of communist society.[4]

Gramsci pointed out that union bureaucracy 'sterilized the creative spirit' and induced a psychology of passivity and deference to authority among workers, who find that the trade union 'has become such an enormous apparatus that it obeys laws internal to its structure' and feel that 'their will for power is not adequately expressed... in the present institutional hierarchy'.[5]

If bureaucratic reformism negated the revolutionary potential of the unions, the working-class parties (notably the PSI) floundered in a political immobility that had developed out of a profound lack of unity and identity. Whereas the unions could never transcend the economic sphere enough to politicize the everyday struggles of workers, the parties were limited by the reverse phenomenon: their narrow world of political involvement (parliament, elections, local administration) made it impossible for them to establish any organic presence in the productive life of the masses. Possessing little beyond a loose electoral relationship with diverse voting constituencies, the PSI was unable to assume firm leadership and became, in Gramsci's words, 'a spectator of the course of events'.[6] With each new electoral success (it gained 32 per cent of the vote and elected 156 deputies in 1919), the PSI fell more and more under the influence of parliamentarians and reformists whose political vision did not go much beyond votes and patronage. Instead of a party of mass mobilization with its own political identity, it became an interest-based, bureaucratized party that had failed to 'acquire its own precise and distinct features'.[7] As the PSI sought to broaden its electoral base it began to sacrifice whatever strategic and ideological coherence it had possessed and became, according to Gramsci, nothing more than a 'conglomeration of forces' lacking compact unity and direction.[8] The impasse of the PSI at the moment of postwar crisis in Italy was therefore predictable enough; like the CGIL, it was not rooted in any revolutionary process outside bourgeois institutions. This mechanical separation of economics and politics encouraged a limited and partial involvement of both unions and parties in their respective spheres.

By early 1919, it had become clear to Gramsci and many other dissidents within the Italian working class movement that neither the PSI nor the trade unions could be salvaged as instruments of revolutionary struggle. The impatience of the Turin group within the PSI had been visible for some time; talk of party 'renewal' gave way to talk of creating entirely new popular organs of socialist struggle. In May

1919 a nucleus of Turin Marxist activists, headed by Gramsci, took the first step when they started the weekly theoretical and political newspaper *L'Ordine Nuovo*. With their critique of trade unions and the established parties as a point of departure, the *Ordinovisti* (who included among their ranks other future PCI intellectuals such as Palmiro Togliatti, Umberto Terracini, and Angelo Tasca) began to articulate a theory of the factory councils – the *consigli di fabbrica* – as the embryonic structure of a new socialist order. *L'Ordine Nuovo* thus became, in the period 1919–1921, the 'paper of the factory councils' and the voice of a movement that stressed the principle of workers' control at the point of production as the basis of a different kind of politics.[9] The councils, as Gramsci put it in his initial *Ordine Nuovo* articles, represented a 'new era of humanity', in which the form and content of socialist society would be prefigured in the ongoing struggle of workers to transform all aspects of their everyday life.

The ideological and practical work of the *Ordinovisti* had its greatest success in Piedmont, where hundreds of councils evolved out of the traditional, union-defined *commissione interne* (internal commissions) after 1919, enlisting the participation of tens of thousands of workers. In Turin, the 30 Fiat plants gave the clearest expression to this new tendency, which by 1921 had transformed the city into a 'Petrograd of Italy', cut off from the mainstream of the PSI as well as the Second International. The council movement had in fact looked to the early stages of the Bolshevik Revolution for its inspiration; the councils were viewed by Gramsci as the germ of future Italian soviets – a nucleus of the socialist state that would lend popular content to the 'dictatorship of the proletariat'. What gave the factory councils particular historical impact was their emergence at a time of powerful revolutionary upsurge throughout Northern Italy; new demands were expressed in the context of widespread strikes, factory occupations, and mass demonstrations. The Turin General Strike of April 1920 forced the issue of workers' control more dramatically than ever, when only massive army intervention was able to stem full-scale proletarian insurrection. For a while the *Ordine Nuovo* movement, situated organically within the working class as it was, thrived in this milieu, but the absence of mass support outside Piedmont and the antagonism of the PSI leadership cut short its development after the autumn of 1920. The political reaction and repression that followed all but obliterated the councils for another twenty years, until they reemerged at the time of the Resistance.

What, then, lives on in the theoretical contributions of Gramsci and the Turin intellectuals who were part of this historically important but ill-fated postwar upheaval? What conception of revolution emerges out of *L'Ordine Nuovo*? Gramsci's initial point of departure, which was consistent with his critique of the CGIL and PSI, was that socialist revolution would have to occur beneath the reality of liberal democractic institutions, as an organic process of creating an entirely new civilization. One of the fallacies of all previous Marxist tendencies had been 'the acceptance of historical reality produced by capitalist initiative', which meant preoccupation with the *existing* state as something to be either seized or transformed. Gramsci insisted that a completely new approach to politics and authority was needed:

> We are persuaded, after the experience of the Russian, Hungarian, and German Revolutions, that the socialist state cannot emerge within the institutions of the capitalist state, but is a fundamentally new creation in relation to them, if not in relation to the history of the proletariat.[10]

Not the *conquest* of power, but a *process* of revolutionary development rooted in the ongoing struggles of workers and culminating in a qualitatively new 'network of proletarian institutions', was the basic premise of Gramsci's theory. Any movement that looks to the old state apparatus in whatever form only succeeds in yielding itself up to the laws of capitalism; it necessarily abandons the autonomous power of the working class itself. Instead of building new forms, it ends up reproducing old ones.

Borrowing from syndicalist and some anarchist thought, Gramsci maintained that an authentic socialism would have to embrace 'two revolutions': one to destroy the bourgeois state and another to transform the capitalist economy. It was in the latter, within the realm of the factory, that the nucleus of the new state would originate. The evolving socialist structures (i.e. councils) would be the medium through which the totality of proletarian existence – its economics and politics, its culture and social relations, its general consciousness – would be gradually transformed. These various aspects of the revolutionary process are not mechanically separated in Gramsci's theory, as they were with the Second International, but are conceptualized in their dialectical unity, so that the factory council as an 'instrument of mortal struggle against capitalism' was not defined – as the unions had been – around strictly economic or contractual objectives. Still, it was at the point of production that all phases of struggle would come together:

> The revolutionary organizations of the political party and the trade union are born on the terrain of political liberty and bourgeois democracy, as an affirmation and development of liberty and of democracy in general, where the relationships of citizen to citizen subsist. The revolutionary process takes place on the terrain of production, in the factory, where the relations are those of oppressor to oppressed, of exploiter to exploited, where freedom for the worker does not exist, where democracy does not exist.[11]

By countering the bureaucratic and contractual legality of the parites and unions, the councils would have greater potential to mobilize the spontaneous impulses of the workers and thus broaden the scope and thrust of rebellion. Gramsci saw in their close relationship to everyday proletarian life a source of popular initiative and psychological awakening that for the first time would give the workers a sense of revolutionary purpose. The councils would be the institutions through which the proletariat could take control of the economy and realize its freedom to create history; in this sense, they would become the primary organs for combating bourgeois hegemony. In Gramsci's words:

> The existence of the councils gives the workers direct responsibility for production, leads them to improve their work, institutes a conscious and voluntary discipline, and creates the psychology of the producer, the creator of history. The workers will carry this new consciousness into the union, and the latter, instead of pursuing the simple activity of the class struggle, will devote itself to the fundamental work of imprinting a new configuration on economic life and labour technique; it will

devote itself to the elaboration of the forms of economic life and professional technique proper to communist civilization.[12]

The factory councils, therefore, represented for Gramsci a new major historical event, the expression of a revolutionary dynamic that had 'exploded into the light of day'. These original forms of workers' self-management were, even in their embryonic state, the repository of a growing sense of dignity, strength, and 'socialist spirit' in all sectors of the work force, affecting through their growth other institutions such as unions and parties, which now had the potential to become the organic representation of popular struggles rather than mechanical impositions of bureaucratic structures. Because of their small size and the democratic involvement of all workers, regardless of skill or union affiliation, the councils could emerge as the primary agencies of collectivity and unity that would make it concretely possible for the proletariat to recover its subjectivity; in Gramsci's words, 'the whole mass participates in the life of the council and feels itself to be something through this activity'.[13] The workers, striving to take control over all aspects of their existence, begin to replace step by step the bourgeois concept of 'citizen' with the revolutionary concept of 'comrade'; the proletariat thereby overcomes its fragmentation, 'acquiring a consciousness of its organic unity and counterposing itself as a whole to capitalism'.[14] The factory council and the principles it embodies unite dialectically structure and consciousness in such a fashion that a previously subdued and divided class is transformed into an active 'single organism'.

From a strictly political point of view, the factory councils would in Gramsci's opinion represent an advance beyond the party in terms of three contributions: (1) they would counter the tendencies towards bureaucratization and Jacobinism in any large-scale organization; (2) they would more effectively preserve the autonomy and identity of the revolutionary movement vis-à-vis bourgeois institutions, and thus help to offset the possibilities of deradicalization that such diverse theorists as Michels, Lenin, Luxemburg, and Sorel had already analyzed in Social Democracy; and (3) they would prefigure in their own development the future socialist state, which 'already exists potentially in the institutions of social life characteristic of the working class'. What unites these three purposes is the central idea of democractic participation within relatively small-scale structures. The councils were indeed the locus of constant meetings, discussions, assemblies, educational and cultural circles, out of which came specific decisions relating to production and a more general preparation for exercising authority in the factory and in the larger society. Gramsci saw in the factory council the germ of the Russian soviet, or peoples' council, in which the principles of proletarian democracy would be generalized beyond the confines of the productive realm itself. As membership and scope increased, the councils would assume the administrative and political functions previously performed by the bourgeois state, first at the local level and then, when the struggle for hegemony had been advanced, at the national level. The Bolshevik slogan 'All Power to the Soviets' therefore made a great amount of strategic sense to Gramsci. The councils, rooted more firmly in the grass-roots existence of the masses, would constitute a far stronger bulwark of democractic participation than any other political form.

The factory councils that did in fact appear in Piedmont during the *Ordine Nuovo* years never actually approximated the theoretical prescription formulated by Gramsci; he always referred to them as the 'nucleus' or 'embryo' of the fully-developed council. Of the hundreds that did emerge, most evolved out of the old union-affiliated internal commissions and these moved only gropingly towards real democratic involvement among all workers. Normally the small labour teams in a plant would elect a representative, or commissar, who would become a member of a plant-wide council of commissars, which in turn would vote to select an executive committee of 3 to 9 members. The principle of delegation held sway, but it was conditioned by open, everyday participation of most workers in the meetings, educational sessions, and demonstrations. At the outset, of course, the councils ran into many obstacles. The opposition of the trade unions and the PSI made recruitment of workers into the councils more difficult and also helped to cut off the *Ordine Nuovo* movement from Central and Southern Italy. Where the councils succeeded in taking over large enterprises, as at Fiat in Turin, immediate problems arose. Most workers lacked expertize in industrial management, but a more overwhelming difficulty stemmed from the attempt to operate specific plants along socialist lines while both the larger economy and the state remained under bourgeois control. On the one hand, there was the problem of obtaining supplies and keeping output high; on the other, there was the recurrent and ultimately fatal reality of police and military repression.

This raises some important questions concerning the general validity of the conception of prefigurative struggle and the role of the councils. For example, what is the historical function of the revolutionary party and what is its relationship to the councils? As we have already suggested, Gramsci's early writings on the party nowhere approach the systematic quality to be found later in the *Prison Notebooks*, or even in his contributions to the Theses of the Lyons Congress in 1926. At times he appeared to adopt a strict Leninist model, while at others his preoccupation with the councils leads him to ignore the function of large-scale organization altogether. The general tenor of the *Ordine Nuovo* writings, however, seems to be in the direction of a broad-based mass party grounded in everyday social life and linked organically to the councils. Certainly Gramsci never, even in his more 'syndicalist' moments, repudiated the idea of a political party that would provide general leadership, theory, and organizational co-ordination for the purpose of popular mobilization and destruction of the bourgeois state machinery. At the same time, he insisted that the party should be nothing more than an expression of proletarian consensus at any given historical period – i.e. that in certain crucial respects (the development of leadership cadres and intellectuals, the formulation of strategy) it must be the *culmination* of mass struggles rather than the *prime mover* itself. The *Ordine Nuovo* articles, for example, often articulated a conception of revolution that stressed the primacy of economics; the workers' struggle for control of production would have to precede the actual contestation for political power, not vice-versa, as Bordiga and the 'centralists' viewed the process.[15] The party assists in moulding this revolutionary development but it does not in any way create it:

> Communist society can only be conceived as a 'natural' formation built on the means of production and exchange: and the revolution can only be conceived as the act of historical acknowledgement of the 'naturalness' of this formation. Hence the revolutionary process can only be identified with a spontaneous movement of the working masses caused by the clash of contradictions inherent in common life under a regime of capitalist property . . . The proletariat's organs of struggle are the 'agents' of this colossal mass movement; the Socialist Party is indubitably the most important 'agent' in this process of destruction and rebuilding, but it is not and cannot be conceived as the form of this process, a form malleable and plastic to the leaders' will.[16]

This organic or 'natural' approach appears often in Gramsci's pre-1922 work and would seem to be in some respects most consistent with his later emphasis upon the struggle for ideological hegemony. And yet, as we shall see in the following chapter, the early focus gradually gives way to its opposite – the primacy of politics – which in the *Prison Notebooks* serves to justify a more autonomous and even 'Jacobin' definition of the party. Had Gramsci in fact done a complete about-face? A close reading of the *Notebooks* (as well as the PCI writings between 1923 and 1926) actually reveals a more complex, dialectical conception of the relationship between economics and politics, councils and party, structures and consciousness. Just as Gramsci did not ignore the role of the party during the *Ordine Nuovo* struggles, neither did he totally abandon his earlier theory of organic transformation in his prison writings. This is what gives Gramsci's political thought so much of its unique richness and depth; he always viewed the revolutionary process as a totality, even though he often chose momentarily to focus his theoretical lenses sharply on one element. What characterized the development of Gramsci's Marxism from its 'early' to 'late' stages was more a change of emphasis in response to new poltical conditions than a total rupture. A point that Gramsci made about understanding Marx's work would seem to apply equally to his own: a theorist must be studied from the perspective of the overall guiding themes and motifs of his writings, within the *totality* of his intellectual evolution, before the specific periods and components can be isolated and compared. In Gramsci, the early elaboration of the strategic importance of councils was organically related to the major elements of his lifetime work – the concept of hegemony and the role of mass consciousness, the notion of 'organic' intellectuals, the theme of prefigurative struggle, and the dialectical interaction between economics and politics.

At the same time, Gramsci's evaluation of the council movement after the Italian failures of 1919–1921 unquestionably began to change; the painful isolation of the Turin councils produced many second thoughts about the efficacy of the 'dual power' approach. From the founding of the Italian Communist Party in early 1921 until the fascist consolidation of power in 1926, Gramsci and the other *Ordinovisti* continued to push a line favouring greater emphasis on the councils, the various workers' and peasants' committees that had emerged throughout Italy, and other potential grass-roots structures that might help to overcome the sectarian, centralist nature of an increasingly-isolated PCI. But Gramsci never sought to obscure his criticism of the factory councils days. The defeats, he felt, were logically tied to an approach that encouraged seizing control of the productive apparatus without simultaneously pressing the issue of state power. Hence, at a time when many factories in Turin and elsewhere were occupied by workers, political and military authority remained firmly in the hands of the bourgeoisie. Lacking its own political force in the way of a party or a peoples' militia, the council movement was easily encircled and finally crushed. Gramsci concluded that, in its syndicalist enthusiasm, *L'Ordine Nuovo* was too confined to the factories. Had there evolved a truly revolutionary party with an experienced leadership capable of universalizing the local proletarian struggles at that moment of crisis, the outcome might have been different. As it was, the militancy and sense of initiative the Italian workers had created through their heroic actions over a period of many months soon became dissipated.[17] This lesson expanded Gramsci's horizons and led him to devote more and more attention to the function of the party, in both theory and practice.

The failure of the council movement to transcend the 'economic-corporate' sphere and build a viable revolutionary movement did not, however, negate for Gramsci its general theoretical implications. The councils did, in fact, raise new issues and instil a new vision in the minds of thousands of workers, who continued to talk about the struggles of the *Ordine Nuovo* period for years afterwards. And the workers in many plants actually did show a capacity for self-management and technical competence that had astonished even themselves. The legacy of the factory occupations and the councils became a feature of proletarian culture in Northern Italy, to emerge later in the form of the Committees for National Liberation (CLNs) during the Resistance and early postwar years, and even later in the form of the *comitati di base* (committees of the base) and other extra-parliamentary groups in the late 1960s. Thus, over a period of five decades, the theory and practice of a popular, anti-bureaucratic, and prefigurative revolutionary movement was kept alive within Italy, as an antidote to ossified, institutionalized structures like the postwar Communist Party.

Historically, therefore, the theoretical-strategic tradition that came out of the council struggles and which was perhaps best articulated in Gramsci's early essays and articles, has perpetuated within Marxism the most vital and hopeful alternative to the one-dimensional, bureaucratic politics of the Third International and other 'vanguard' tendencies. Integrating some of the concepts and experiences of the anarchist, anarcho–syndicalist, and 'council communist' movements, but going beyond them, prefigurative Marxism has raised the question of political power and bureaucracy in the historical context of a whole series of confrontations: the anti-authoritarian opposition to Leninism and Stalinism in Russia during the 1920s, the rise of the councils and the 'ultra-left' opposition to the Comintern in Germany and elsewhere during the same period, the vast expansion of 'dual power' structures during the Spanish Civil War, the aforementioned explosion of the council movement in Italy between 1943 and 1947, and the emergence of the new left and extraparliamentary struggles (typified by the French Revolt of May 1968) in the 1960s. In all of these cases, new kinds of questions were asked – similar to the ones Gramsci had posed at the time of *L'Ordine Nuovo*: what are the forms and structures of authority appropriate to socialism, and how can they be embodied in present, ongoing, everyday activity? By tackling these issues head on, the various council movements sought to counter the fetishism of organization and centralized leadership, the obsession with the conquest of state power, and the equation of economic planning with socialism that has been the defining character of most self-styled Leninist parties in the twentieth century.

Yet Gramsci's theory, when viewed in its totality, was ultimately much more dialectical in its attempt to link the organic spontaneous, everyday sphere with the universal realm of politics and the revolutionary party. Gramsci shared with the anarchists and prefigurative Marxists like Kropotkin, Pannekoek, and Gorter a commitment to transforming authority and social relations, production and work, culture and life-styles through the construction of small, local organs of socialist democracy as the *pre-condition* for achieving a qualitatively new order and a new state – in Gramsci's words, a new 'integrated culture'. Gramsci also shared with these theorists a conception of subverting the institutions and values of bourgeois society by attacking their manifestation in all aspects of everyday life, by demystifying established authority in the context of asserting popular control throughout civil society – i.e. by eroding the myriad expressions of ideological hegemony. And he agreed that revolutionary change would ultimately have to come from the self-conscious initiative of the masses themselves, working through structures like the councils in rebellion against *all* forms of authoritarian control, rather than hierarchical bodies like the parties and trade unions. Yet Gramsci departed from this tradition, increasingly over time, out of his growing conviction that socialism could never be realized without the intervention of an 'external' mediator (the revolutionary party) that could impart unity and political-military force to diverse spontaneous struggles. His overriding concern was to synthesize the two levels rather than to contrast them – to bring together the organizational and spontaneous, the political and economic, the party and councils. Gramsci's critique of the anarchists and anarcho-syndicalists, for example, was based on their 'undialectical' approach to the problem of power; whereas they viewed all macrostructures as bureaucratic and reactionary by definition, Gramsci thought it possible to ground a vastly different kind of party – an authentic *mass party* – in the tradition of the councils. The collapse of *L'Ordine Nuovo* resulting from its political isolation taught Gramsci a lesson in this respect.

The overall revolutionary strategy that emerges from Gramsci's thought, while never clearly outlined at any single point in his writings, lends concrete, structural content to his theoretical attempt to transcend the extremes of spontaneism and Jacobinism. It is a strategy that comprehends socialist transformation as a process emerging out of grass-roots democratic structures that give shape to the party and prepare the ground for dismantling the old state apparatus while creating an entirely different kind of political order in its place. More than any other Marxist of his time, Gramsci articulated a prefigurative conception of struggle that advanced a new model of public life — one that emphasized the *simultaneous* overturning of economic production relations, political decision-making, culture and social life, i.e. the transformation of the entire social division of labour under capitalism. Above all, a prefigurative movement meant that politics would be integrated into the everyday social existence of people struggling to change the world, so that the elitism, authoritarianism, and impersonal style typical of bureaucracy could be more effectively combated. Central to this problematic are two broad themes that permeate Gramsci's Marxism but which are never fully developed in his work: that socialism must embody popular control of all spheres of human life, and that it must give expression to a completely new kind of state.

5. The Revolutionary Party: 'Modern Prince' and 'Collective Intellectual'

It has often been remarked that the nineteenth century was above all a period of general hostility toward politics, of a turning away from issues related to public power, the state, and collective action in the aftermath of the French Revolution.[1] Certainly Marxism no less than liberalism was a product of this anti-political trend, which encouraged a reduction of the political realm to the more 'basic' level of social and economic phenomena. Insofar as politics was taken into account by theorists at all, it was treated as the expression of larger historical forces, and rarely as something having its own distinct existence within a total complex of institutions and social relationships. In Marxism – despite what Marx said about Feuerbach being 'too much concerned with nature and too little with politics' – there had been from the start a theoretical preoccupation with the economic 'substructure' to the exclusion of the 'superstructure'. Marx himself never really got around to developing a systematic theory of politics and the state, which left a void that encouraged a tendency towards economic determinism by the time of the Second International.

Marx's early writings, with the memory of the Jacobin terror in France still vivid, revealed a strong antagonism to politics; he considered the attempt to impose a new political order upon a civil society not yet ready to undergo fundamental change as destined either to fail or to lead to new forms of centralized coercion. Politics, Marx felt, could never serve as a prime mover. Socialist transformation would have to be the fulfilment of the potentialities inherent in socio-economic development, a process in which new political organizations and structures would have to be organically rooted in civil society. The Blanquists, conspiratorial sects, and other 'alchemists of revolution' had failed to understand this. Marx's distrust of politics in this sense was understandable enough, but his overall failure to integrate it dialectically into his revolutionary theory would be one of the main factors in the later decline of European Marxism. Having developed no systematic conception of the bourgeois state or of the kind of revolutionary structures that would replace it, – indeed, having paid little attention to 'superstructural' concerns at all – the later variants of Marxism easily fell prey to economism, spontaneism, and positivism. Insofar as the primacy of economics was held sacrosanct, political strategy itself was never considered a central problem since politics itself could hardly be envisaged as a positive, creative instrument of revolutionary change.

But if nineteenth century theory stressed the primacy of the 'substructure', surely twentieth-century history has given expression to its opposite – the primacy of politics. The rise of fascism, the transformation of competitive capitalism into state corporate capitalism, and the appearance of Third World military dictatorships have all seriously called into question the classical Marxist approach to politics.

It was Lenin, of course, who first reversed this order of priorities within Marxism itself by stressing the role of politics over economics both in his theoretical work and in his leadership of the Bolshevik party. Lenin departed from classical theory by insisting that any movement that confined itself to economic struggle could never transcend the logic of prevailing structures; to counter that logic (i.e. to become revolutionary), a movement would have to express its negation of the system in *political* terms. Economism encouraged a narrow, particularistic vision that in working-class struggles often led to an interest-group focus, whereas politics generally raised conflict to the level of the public, common, and collective, thus providing the arena for realizing the ideological goals of socialism that could give larger shape to concrete material demands. More specifically, politics for Lenin meant building an instrument of collective action – an organized party – the overriding purpose of which was the conquest of state power for revolutionary objectives. Politics, in this sense, was conceived of as a powerful mechanism for (a) mobilizing the masses, (b) seizing power and establishing a 'dictatorship of the proletariat', and (c) constructing socialism in the post-revolutionary period. The Leninist party was thus designed to maxmize leadership mobility and political identity during the struggle for power, thus allowing for the most effective intervention at the moment of crisis in the traditional order. Lenin's strategy – criticized as 'ultra-politicism' by Paul Axelrod and 'Blanquism' by Rosa Luxemburg – was an extreme assertion of the political in the sense of urgency it conveyed and in the degree of initiative it gave to a relatively small elite of professional revolutionaries. It may well have been that this 'minority revolution' variant of Marxist strategy, to use Stanley Moore's term,[2] was the inevitable consequence of Lenin's initial 'discovery' of politics that was dictated by the deficiencies in classical Marxism and by the autocratic nature of Russian society.

The Leninist vision of revolutionary struggle and its embodiment in the Bolshevik Revolution made a deep impression upon Gramsci, although he did not take up the primacy of politics theme in earnest until some time after the collapse of *L'Ordine Nuovo* – not until the later stages of his PCI involvement and particularly his prison writings. What Gramsci set out to do was to build on Leninism by extending it and adding another dimension to it. Lenin's breakthrough opened up enormous new theoretical and political opportunities in European Marxism, which Gramsci was amongst the first to grasp. He readily accepted Lenin's devastating critique of economism and his notion that politics was the key to revolutionary struggle, but, confronting different conditions and a new historical situation in Western Europe, he sought to incorporate the 'popular' element that, as we have already seen, was integral to his preoccupation with the problem of mass consciousness. While Gramsci probably devoted greater theoretical attention to the distinctly political realm of struggle than any other Marxist, including Lenin, he nonetheless always insisted upon a 'dual perspective', or totality, that prevented politics from taking on Leviathan proportions.

The shift from Gramsci's emphasis upon the role of the factory councils to his preoccupation with politics and the revolutionary party was already visible by 1920–1921, at the time of the founding of the PCI, and became more pronounced after 1924, when Mussolini was consolidating his power and the PCI was forced to struggle for its survival. With the collapse of the council movement and the spread of reaction in Italy, Gramsci gradually turned his interest towards the bourgeois state itself and the role of the Marxist party in its overthrow. Only through the centralized leadership and organized unity of the working class, acting not only in the factories and economic sphere but in the political arena as well, could socialism now be put on the agenda.[3] The Leninist model that had inspired the creation of the PCI appeared more and more attractive to Gramsci, not merely as a means of combating fascism but as an instrument for undercutting reformism too.

At first, Gramsci argued that the party ought to be the organic expression of 'intermediary' popular structures such as the workers' councils and soviets; by 1923–1924, however, following his return from Russia, he made less mention of the councils and began stressing the primary role of the revolutionary party as the 'protagonist of history'.[4] He praised Lenin's strategy and tactics in a number of articles, attacked the reformist division of labour between party and trade unions characteristic of the PSI, and urged the PCI to adopt a policy of mass mobilization based upon a system of cells – the small-scale, basic party organizations that had been introduced by the Bolsheviks.[5] This also meant abandoning the old social-democratic illusions of the 'parliamentary road' to socialism, which died hard in Italy as elsewhere in Western Europe. By 1926, Gramsci was convinced more than ever that the political identity of what remained of Italian revolutionary socialism could be preserved only through a Leninist party committed to an *offensive* posture against *both* bourgeois and fascist institutions.

But Gramsci's Leninism, even at this desperate point in Italian politics, never assumed the narrow, one-sided, and extremely voluntarist conception of the revolutionary process normally associated with the vanguard party. Throughout the early and mid-1920s, he never turned his back on the positive experiences of the *Ordine Nuovo* period or on his earlier theoretical interest in hegemony and mass consciousness; if the party now took on a new dialectical importance, this did not signify endorsement of it alone as the vehicle of transition. Gramsci insisted upon a *mass* party, its leadership rooted in everyday working-class and peasant life, prepared to operate in all spheres of bourgeois society. His ongoing debate with Bordiga was over precisely these issues: whether the PCI should be the co-ordinator or the initiator of popular struggles, whether centralism and organizational integrity should be maintained to the point of abstentionism (Bordiga's position), whether the struggle for state power was the immediate and overriding task of the party (as Bordiga assumed), etc. In rejecting Bordiga's concept of a narrow vanguard party, Gramsci once again stressed the principle of totality, which explicitly informed his notion of the primacy of politics developed in the *Prison Notebooks*. Thus, in 1925 Gramsci identified *three* main phases of the struggle against capital – the economic, political, and cultural-ideological – each phase interrelated with the others in the complex totality of revolutionary transition, and each phase itself embracing several dimensions.[6]

Yet as we have seen, politics occupies a very special place in Gramsci's theory, especially in his prison writings. While he never disavows the totalistic perspective in the *Prison Notebooks*, he does return repeatedly to the political as a favourite theme, motivated no doubt less by his infatuation with the strict Leninst sense of the primacy of politics than by his passionate desire to rescue politics from its dismal fate within classical Marxism. Therefore, what Gramsci wanted to do, given the anti-political and economic determinist bias of socialist theory, was to make a case for the distinctly political as a 'language' of communication, a mode of analysis, and an instrument of revolutionary change. But instead of reversing the traditional schema by substituting a *political* determinism or crude voluntarism for economism, he concentrated upon politics merely to the extent of restoring the Marxist totality. In Gramsci's view, Marxism had forgotten that in the broad Aristotelian conception human beings are fundamentally political by nature: 'To transform the external world, the general system of relations, is to potentiate oneself and to develop oneself.' Hence: ' – one can say that man is essentially "political" since it is through the activity of transforming and consciously directing other men that man realizes his "humanity", his "human nature".'[7] Moreover, in positing a social development governed by 'scientific' laws of motion, Marxism had also permitted the concept of the state and the political to degenerate; the diverse elements of the superstructure were left to themselves, to develop spontaneously in the manner of a 'haphazard and sporadic germination'.[8]

Gramsci noted that the primacy of economics in orthodox Marxism tended to undermine the search for political solutions to the contradictions of bourgeois society. It often posed the right questions, but within a limited and simplistic framework that could lead only to a theoretical and practical immobility:

> Confronted with [historical political] events, economism asks the question: 'who profits directly from the initiative under consideration?' and replies with a line of reasoning which is as simplistic as it is fallacious: the ones who profit directly are a certain fraction of the ruling class . . . This sort of infallibility comes very cheaply. It not only has no theoretical significance – it has only minimal implications for practical efficacy. In general, it produces nothing but moralistic sermons, and interminable questions of personality.[9]

In contrast to the economists, Gramsci argued that 'the search for appropriate means to control in practice the overall political strategy will always remain of exclusively political competence . . .'[10] It was this compelling interest in the political sphere that attracted Gramsci so much to the theory of Machiavelli, whose nearly obsessive desire to see the unification of sixteenth century Italy inspired him to seek a solution in the universalizing and collective potential of political authority. Gramsci often referred to Machiavelli as the 'first Jacobin' and praised him as a theorist who wanted to combine historical understanding with a strong commitment to creating a new human community through political action. Thus:

> In his treatment, in his critique of the present, he expressed general concepts . . . and an original conception of the world. This conception of the world too could be called 'philosophy of praxis', or 'neo-humanism' [which] bases itself entirely on the concrete action of man, who, impelled by historical necessity, works and transforms reality.

Gramsci adds to this: 'But what Machiavelli does do is to bring everything back to politics – i.e. to the art of governing men, of securing their permanent consent, and hence of founding "great states".'[11]

This ability to capture the essence of politics and to recognize its special domain was, in Gramsci's view, Machiavelli's great contribution. The painstaking study of historical forces was for Machiavelli a main point of departure; but the true 'statesman', or prince, never confines his attention to 'effective reality' but seeks to understand the present and future as part of the total historical process. He utilizes politics – the only truly 'common' realm – to establish a new relation of forces, a new homogeneous order. Gramsci's interpretation of Machiavelli in the *Prison Notebooks* was that he was much less concerned with the static world of descriptive social 'reality' (i.e. 'objective' conditions) than with the mechanism for transforming that reality (politics), and that whereas the former led to narrow, immediate preoccupations, the latter opened up the potential for initiative, foresight, and long-range vision. Since Machiavelli believed this was the only space in which truly collective issues related to the popular will could be raised, let alone resolved, politics became the vehicle for creating unity and sense of community where there had been only fragmentation and conflict – as the case of the Italian city-states. Politics was what propelled human beings forward to some new ideal, what enabled them to 'dominate' reality as part of understanding it. Gramsci saw Machiavelli as

> ... not merely a scientist: he was a partisan, a man of powerful passions, an active politician, who wishes to create a new balance of forces and therefore cannot help concerning himself with what 'ought to be' ...
>
> The active politician is a creator, an initiator; but he neither creates from nothing nor does he move in the turbid void of his own desires and dreams. He bases himself on effective reality, but what is this effective reality? Is it something static and immobile, or is it not rather a relation of forces in continuous motion and shift of equilibrium? If one applies one's will to the creation of a new equilibrium among the forces which really exist and are operative – basing oneself on the practical force which one believes to be progressive and strengthening it to help it to victory – one still moves on the terrain of effective reality, but do so in order to dominate and transcend it (or to contribute to this). What 'ought to be' is therefore concrete; indeed it is the only realistic and

historicist interpretation of reality, it alone is history in the making, it alone is politics.[12]

What Marxism lacked, Gramsci argued, was precisely this Machiavellian theory and art of statecraft that aims not so much at 'knowledge of men' or 'disinterested scientific activity' as at 'connecting seemingly disparate facts' and laying down the 'means adequate to particular ends'.[13] Thus politics must be equally as concerned with arousing popular passions, with activating the collective will as with discovering various forms of knowledge or logic; the *Prince*, for example, was a 'live' theoretical work, combining historical generalizations with the appeal of 'myth'. 'Such a procedure stimulates the artistic imagination of those who have to be convinced, and gives political passions a more concrete form.'[14] At several points Gramsci drew parallels between Machiavelli's 'prince' and Sorel's 'myth' – both being emotive agents of mass mobilization. Machiavelli's was neither the 'cold theorizing' of Plato's utopia nor the 'learned discourse' of Locke's treatises, but the creative instrument of collective transformation in which politics functions primarily to *transcend* the existing order of things. His was 'the style of a man of action, of a man urging action, the style of a party manifesto'.[15]

The concrete meaning of politics in Gramsci's Marxism, then, was its role in enlisting mass energies in the struggle for ideological hegemony and in establishing a new socialist 'national-popular' community out of the cleavages and crises of the old society. Politics constituted the arena of collective struggle that transcends the parochial interests of particular constituencies and imparts identity and cohesion to the process of socialist transformation. The difficulty with Sorel's myth was that, in relying heavily on the spontaneous vital impulse of Bergson's *élan vital*, it left no room for the planned, 'conscious' element. At the same time, Croce's vision of a new Italian culture emerging strictly out of changes within the 'ethico-political' sphere was deficient in that it lacked any conception of structural transformation. Lenin's type of Jacobinism, moreover, was *elitist* and authoritarian to the extent that it envisaged the revolutionary transition as a project defined and led by a tightly-organized nucleus of professional cadres.

What Gramsci outlined was neither an anarchistic spontaneous mass movement nor an *elite* party that would be the exclusive repository of consciousness, but a synthesis of the two – an organic linkage between *elite* and mass, the organized and spontaneous, the planned element and the vital impulse. It was the function of politics therefore to create a socialist identity by 'universalizing' diverse struggles, but by 'leading' (providing 'intellectual-moral' guidance and inspiration) rather than by organizational compulsion. Gramsci's Jacobinism thus contained a 'popular' or consensual component that was not normally associated with the primacy of politics.[16]

Politics, for Gramsci as for Machiavelli, asserts the role of the conscious element over spontaneism, the emotive and partisan element over value-free detachment, and the common or public element over the particular. It embodies the maturity of a revolutionary movement that begins to transcend the limited, fragmented, and often conflicting 'corporate' demands of diverse constituencies. This universalizing force was the one mechanism that could unite an historically-divided Italy and stimulate progressive change; the regional, economic, and religious cleavages of Machiavelli's time not only persisted into the twentieth century but were intensified and compounded by the peculiarly uneven development of Italian capitalism. Gramsci quickly grasped the importance of this theme for revolutionary politics, especially as it applied to the growing socio-economic lag of the South behind the North (what Gramsci, after Gaetano Salvemini, called the 'Southern question'). In addition, Gramsci noted that advanced levels of capitalist development led to a growing diversification of the working class itself – a tendency that was already visible in the North – making a unified socialist identity more imperative than ever. Increased complexity, specialization, and atomization of the labour force means increased differentiation in wages, status, life-styles, and culture, and hence potentially a variety of localized movements pursuing their own interests and following their own dynamic. To counter these centrifugal forces would be a major task of the Marxist revolutionary party; the PCI, as Gramsci saw it, would have to forge a 'revolutionary historical bloc' out of the very cleavages and contradictions of Italian society.

Gramsci's strategic interest in politics as a mediating instrument did not so much negate economic struggles as seek to establish a dialectical relationship between the two spheres of politics and economics – a dynamic conception that had been absent from traditional Marxism. To the extent that workers' struggles were confined to economic issues within the factory they tended to revolve around the immediate principles of self-interest and material stability, and therefore could only move in the direction of pressure-group type bargaining within the capitalist order. Economism in this sense was from Gramsci's standpoint a *reflection* of the very premises of bourgeois society, a mirroring of the natural order of things under capitalism – a strategy that tended to lose any real 'capacity for cultural expansion'. The ultimate consequence of all forms of economism, syndicalism included, was to restrict popular movements and keep them from contesting hegemony:

> Here we are dealing with a subaltern group which is prevented by this theory from ever becoming dominant, or from developing beyond the economic-corporate stage and rising to the phase of ethical-political hegemony in civil society, and domination of the state.[17]

Gramsci concluded that an external mediating force (politics) would be necessary to raise discrete movements of revolt to the level of real counter-hegemonic struggle, rendering total and qualitative the fundamental conflicts of class society and transforming 'partial' demands into revolutionary ones that challenge the very existence of class oppression and hierarchical authority relations. It would supply a creative initiative, with its own impulse 'above' the parochial nature of popular interest-group consciousness – a form of Jacobinism that overcomes the pragmatism of common sense and opposes the general tendency to confine economic and social aims to the realm of piecemeal reforms. This transformative quality of politics is vital since

> One of the commonest totems is the belief about everything that exists, that it is 'natural' that it should exist . . . and that however badly one's attempts to reform may go they will not stop life going on, since the traditional forces will continue to operate and precisely will keep life

going on . . . One may say that no real movement becomes aware of its global character all at once, but only gradually through experience – in other words, when it learns from the facts that nothing which exists is natural . . . but rather exists because of certain conditions.[18]

Such a 'global' force, however, was always absent in Italian history – a phenomenon that both Machiavelli and Gramsci clearly recognized. There had never been a 'Jacobinism' capable of transcending the divisive cleavages and linking the elite stratum with the popular strata, as was true of the French Revolution. In Italy, as we have seen, no hegemonic political element, including the bourgeoisie of the post-Risorgimento period, succeeded in stirring the passions of the people enough to create anything resembling a national-popular community; the bourgeois liberal revolution, inspired and undertaken largely by a narrow stratum of Piedmont entrepreneurs and intellectuals, was an unfinished process that did not begin to penetrate the old Papal strongholds, the *Mezzogiorno*, or Sicily. No unified set of national beliefs, no nation-state, had ever really evolved in Italy, whereas in France the emergence of 'positive elements' made unification a realizable goal. While in Italy such a political force never emerged, in France it became an 'audacious, dauntless' Jacobinism that represented not the momentary needs of the masses but the historical vision of a community.[19] In France, as in England, the United States, and many other European countries, the state came to embody a universal scope of legitimacy – the kind of ethical and cultural 'spirit' that Croce saw as central to political development. The impediments caused by the awesome power of the Catholic Church made Italy somewhat unique in this respect.

But insofar as this 'supremacy of the political moment' had not appeared in Italy, it provided new historical opportunities for Marxism that were not commonly present elsewhere, and it was one of Gramsci's most valuable insights to perceive this potentially 'national' role of socialist movements (particularly for the PCI) in twentieth-century Italy. Put simply, Gramsci's conception was that the failure of the bourgeoisie to carry out the 'national' revolution gave Marxists an opportunity to do so on their own terms, without waiting for capitalism to run its full course of development. The very weaknesses of bourgeois society that gave rise to the perpetual crises in the Italian political order from the 1870s on actually presented crucial advantages to Marxism, insofar as it was not hampered by a fatalistic determinism that encouraged a passive stance. The 'second Risorgimento', as Gramsci viewed it, would be a communist extension of the first, culminating in absolute rather than partial ideological hegemony, through the organic linkage between a Marxist leadership stratum and the general Italian population and the breaking down of barriers between North and South. This last dynamic was central, for it meant creating an alliance between the Northern proletariat and the Southern peasantry within a 'global' movement that would finally bring an end to the colonial, semi-feudal subjugation of the *Mezziogiorno* by Northern industrial interests. It opened up a dialectic that, by the time of the Lyons Congress in early 1926, became the cornerstone of Gramsci's Marxist strategy, fusing together his conceptions of the primacy of politics, the national task of the PCI, and the 'revolutionary historical bloc'. The demanding process of building a new Italian community, under Marxist hegemony, was dependent upon this resolution of the 'Southern question', since 'any formation of a national-popular collective will is impossible unless the great mass of peasant farmers burst simultaneously into political life'.[20]

If the orthodox Marxists of the pre-First World War PSI had failed to understand this special feature of Italian history, and if the left in general had never taken up the Machiavellian theme of a unified political community, the PCI in the 1920s was hardly more advanced: it too had failed to creatively insert itself into the Italian historical context. Much of this immobility stemmed from the fact that, under Bordiga's leadership, the PCI asserted 'proletarian internationalism' in a way that excluded any national focus. For Bordiga, the PCI appeared at times as an extension of the international communist movement, which meant that as far as theory, strategy, and tactics were concerned, the Italian Party was little more than an appendage of the Comintern. As far as Gramsci was concerned, it was Bordiga's insistence upon placing the Comintern above the PCI that undermined the party's capacity to inspire mass support. Bordiga overlooked the fact that for Marxism to achieve a *popular* foundation in any society it must ultimately be defined in *national* terms that seek to make sense of a particular culture, language, and set of traditions; internationalism in the sense of revolutionary solidarity was of course vital, but internationalism in the sense of universal models was politically harmful. Or, to put it another way:

> In reality, the internal relations of any nation are the result of a combination which is 'original' and (in a certain sense) unique: these relations must be conceived and understood in their originality and uniqueness if one wishes to dominate them and direct them. To be sure, the line of development is towards internationalism, but the point of departure is 'national' – and it is from this point of departure that one must begin. Yet the perspective is international and cannot be otherwise.[21]

Gramsci added that in cases where a rigid form of internationalism was employed, as with the Second International, passivity and inertia developed since 'nobody believed they ought to make a start – that is to say, they believed that by making a start they would find themselves isolated; they waited for everybody to move together, and nobody in the meantime moved or organized the movement'. Similarly, he attacked the later Stalinist concept of 'Socialism in One Country', which advanced the strategy of diffusing the revolution from a single political centre, as an 'anti-natural form of Napoleonism'.[22] Moreover, in response to Bordiga, who argued that national factors could play a role only in colonized countries like Russia, Gramsci countered that the increasing significance of ideological struggle within civil society in the advanced capitalist systems would make it necessary for Marxists to integrate unique historical and cultural factors into their politics. For: 'It is in the concept of hegemony that those exigencies which are national in character are knotted together.'[23] But in the 1920s it was neither the PSI nor the PCI which mobilized this 'national-popular' potential; it was in fact the right, led by Mussolini and the fascists, that possessed the ingenuity to do so. Not until the Resistance of 1943–1945, when massive upheavals against the fascist regime and the German occupation produced an influx of more than two million members into the PCI, did

Italian Marxism begin to assume the national role Gramsci assigned to it in the *Prison Notebooks*.

By linking together the idea of a 'national-popular' movement and the notion of a counter-hegemonic ideological struggle directed by a modern party, Gramsci was able to impart coherent theoretical meaning to both the Machiavellian dream of a unified Italy and the Leninist principle of the primary of politics. This synthesis constituted a major break from traditional theory, both Italian and Marxist in general, and represented a leap beyond even Leninism itself. Whereas Machiavelli wrote about the unifying and regenerative powers of the prince, Gramsci incorporated this concrete embodiment of politics into his conception of an organized revolutionary party that would provide leadership in building socialism. Thus:

> If one had to translate the notion 'Prince', as used in Machiavelli's work, into modern political language, one would have to make a series of distinctions: the 'Prince' could be head of state, or leader, of a government, but it could also be a political leader whose aim is to conquer a state, or to found a new type of state; in this sense, 'Prince' could be translated in modern terms as 'political party'.[24]

The Marxist party, accordingly, is an indispensable co-ordinating force and catalyst – a 'myth prince' that binds together the collective will and functions as the bearer of historical continuity in the development of popular struggles.

That Gramsci's model of revolutionary transformation departed significantly from Lenin's is the direct consequence of Gramsci's emphasis upon ideological hegemony and the national task of Marxism. At the core of these crucial differences is Gramsci's 'dual perspective', rooted in the dichotomy between force and consent in politics, which he conceptualized in terms of 'organic' and 'conjunctural' dimensions of change. By 'conjunctural' Gramsci meant the passing and momentary period of crisis in which the contesting political forces struggle for state power – a stage roughly equivalent to his strategic concept 'war of movement' or 'war of manœuvre'. This was the realm of historical contingency, unpredictability (*fortuna* in Machiavelli's language), tactical decision-making, and of course military confrontation. It was for this arena of political activity and combat that Lenin's highly-centralized party of professional revolutionaries was primarily designed.

The 'organic' aspect of political struggle, on the other hand, referred to the long-range contestation for ideological hegemony, to the gradual shifting in the equilibrium of social forces that must precede the 'conjunctural' moment – what Gramsci called the 'war of position'. This was the 'moral-intellectual' phase of revolutionary development, in which the role of the party was essentially 'cultural-ideological' rather than 'political' in the narrower sense of the struggle for state power. Gramsci's strategy, as opposed to Lenin's, stresses *both* the 'organic' and the 'conjunctural' aspects of politics (e.g. the party is seen as both 'collective intellectual' and 'modern prince'), which points to a revolutionary process infinitely more complex and multi-dimensional, and with more of a popular or consensual basis, than emerged from the classical Leninist model of 'minority revolution'. Although Gramsci never explicitly singled out Lenin for criticism, he consistently rejected that kind of Marxism (e.g. Bordiga's) which equated politics and revolutionary activity with the 'conjunctural'. When looked at from this perspective, the focus of Lenin's party appears one-dimensional: almost exclusive stress placed upon military-political struggle, the role of large-scale organization, the tasks of seizing state power, etc. It is a model geared, strategically and organizationally, to the superimposition of a new order from above, which cannot help but take on a mechanistic and *elitist* character. The Gramscian model, on the other hand, was dialectical in that it specified a reciprocal interaction between the 'organic' and 'conjunctural', and between the party and the larger complex of social groups which make up the total milieu.

This conception of totality is what distinguishes Gramsci's theory of the revolutionary party most clearly. What he articulated in the *Prison Notebooks*, and to a lesser extent in the later PCI writings, was a model of political organization rooted in everyday social life and formed organically through popular struggle, rather than a strict primacy of politics (or the party) over the social sphere. Hence:

> The history of a party, in other words, can only be the history of a particular social group. But this group is not isolated; it has friends, kindred groups, opponents, enemies. The history of any given party can only emerge from the complex portrayal of society and state.[25]

All of this was in Gramsci's theoretical framework closely bound up with the idea of a complex dialectical relationship between 'structure' and 'superstructure', between economics and politics (or the 'ethico-political'), and between organization and consciousness – simply another expression of the 'dual perspective'. To emphasize a single element in the revolutionary process, instead of seeing each bound up in a dialectical totality, would inevitably rob Marxism of its strategic unity and lead either to impasse or 'bureaucratic centralism'.[26] This approach is consistent with Gramsci's philosophy, as outlined above in Chapter 1, and with his understanding of mass consciousness, as discussed in Chapter 3.

What Gramsci had in mind by 'primacy of politics' was therefore something vastly different from Lenin's theory, though it was motivated by many of the same criticisms of orthodox Marxism. For Gramsci, politics was deeply embedded in all aspects of collective revolutionary struggle, beyond the actual contestation for state power itself; as part of the 'ensemble of relations', it was neither an epiphenomenon nor an all-powerful prime mover. Gramsci's theoretical objective was to specify the uniqueness of the political dynamic without at the same time raising it above the totality and rupturing the overall unity of Marxism. In comparison, whatever its other major accomplishments, Leninism appears one-sided and undialectical in its mechanical assertion of political structures over the *ensemble* of relations. Lenin's fixation on the 'conjunctural' had a political as well as theoretical impact, of course, for it opened the door to a dangerous form of Jacobinism that would eventually negate the prospects for socialism itself. In its most extreme form, it would lead to what Gramsci called 'volunteer action' – a dramatic military strategy that looks for rapid success but in the end constitutes a 'surrogate for popular intervention' and thus winds up accepting the passivity of the masses. It also directed far too much attention to the element of crisis, which obscures the immense complexity of civil society and encourages organizational solutions to the problem of hegemony. Gramsci insisted that such a conception, though quite tempting, could only produce a one-dimensional framework that raises elites over masses, organization over ideology, and force over consent, the inevitable outcome being the triumph of means over ends. Without the 'organic' sphere of revolutionary struggle, 'socialism' would rapidly degenerate into a rhetorical ideology employed by a new stratum of elites to perpetuate their power. The oppressed classes themselves must ultimately make history – not political elites, even where these elites claim to be setting the stage for future socialist development. It must be a complex and two-way process.

> ... there is voluntarism or Garibaldism conceived as the initial moment of an organic period which must be prepared and developed; a period in which the organic collectivity, as a social bloc, will participate fully. 'Vanguards' without armies to back them up, 'commandos' without infantry or artillery, these too are transpositions from the language of rhetorical heroism – though vanguard and commandos as specialized functions within complex and regular organisms are quite another thing. The same distinction can be made between the notion of intellectual *elites* separated from the masses, and that of intellectuals who are conscious of being linked organically to a national-popular mass. In reality, one has to struggle against the above-mentioned degenerations, the false heroisms and psuedo-aristocracies, and stimulate the formation of homogeneous, compact social blocs, which will give birth to their own intellectuals, their own commandos, their own vanguard – who in turn will react upon those blocs in order to develop them, and not merely so as to perpetuate their gypsy domination.[27]

This typically Gramscian passage reveals in poetic form a conception of the Marxist party that is as much the *expression* as it is the *mobilizer* of popular struggles. Its ongoing political functions are largely 'indirect' in that they are built around 'leading', guiding, education, raising new issues, etc. in the broadest sense of ideological attack upon bourgeois society. The archetypical political actor is an integral part of the social and economic milieu, firmly rooted in the cultural norms of the larger setting, in contrast to the full-time professional revolutionary of Lenin's vanguard party. It follows that, in Gramsci's model, extra-party structures and activities (e.g. the media, educational groups, counter-hegemonic bodies such as workers' councils and soviets) play a far greater role than the party itself during the 'organic' phase of transformation. This makes possible an organizational dynamic based upon 'organic centralism' – leadership and authority with a collective, consensual support – as opposed to 'bureaucratic centralism', which rests upon hierarchical structures and command.

The implications for Marxist strategy that Gramsci's extension of Leninism has had, or is yet likely to have in the future, become more apparent with the passing of time. The Bolshevik Revolution, which Gramsci himself lauded as the 'decisive turning point in history', has moved steadily away from its original Marxist objectives and stands today as a new type of authoritarian regime defined precisely by the 'bureaucratic centralism' Gramsci had feared. This is no mere 'betrayal' on the part of the CPSU leadership, for while all aspects of the contemporary Soviet system cannot be traced back to the Russian Revolution, the main tendencies do in fact have their origins in Leninist political strategy. Though Gramsci himself was never in a position to do his own systematic analysis of Soviet development, the theories he formulated in the *Prison Notebooks* clearly suggest such a critique, in the context of furnishing an alternative model of revolutionary organization and strategy.

Epilogue:
Gramsci's Marxism Today

The theoretical work that Gramsci was able to complete before his death in 1937 represents one of the truly impressive intellectual and personal achievements in the history of Marxism. Increasingly, the *Prison Notebooks* have been widely recognized as one of the major contributions to modern revolutionary thought, with an influence far beyond Italy and even Western Europe. From the perspective of the 1970s, in the wake of the new left and extra-parliamentary revolts that took place in most of the advanced capitalist societies, Gramsci's thought takes on added significance because it was an innovative part of the 'underground' tradition that kept alive an authentic, critical Marxism through the deformations of Stalinism, the Popular Front, and the post-war deradicalization of mass Communist Parties.[1] Along with Korsch, Lukacs, Reich, Marcuse and the Frankfurt School, Gramsci helped to furnish the general outline of an alternative to the limited theoretical and strategic models of the Second and Third Internationals, but with more of a *political* focus than these other Marxists. Gramsci's creative and dialectical philosophy, his innovative concept of ideological hegemony and his sensitivity to the hidden dimension of mass consciousness, his emphasis upon the councils, dual power, and prefigurative struggle, his totalistic conception of the revolutionary process – all this constitutes an expansive theory of cultural revolution that, unfortunately, was never developed in any systematic way in his writings of the 1920s and 1930s. The belated 'discovery' of Gramsci by many new left intellectuals and political groups in the United States and Western Europe is understandable in the context of a number of striking parallels between Gramscian theory and new left *practice*.

Both Gramsci and the 'underground' Marxist tradition can now be seen more clearly as part of a transitional stage in the intellectual and political development of the European left, extending between the paradigm of classical Marxism and the new problematic of creating a revolutionary praxis for transforming advanced capitalism. The fact that Gramsci was never able to escape this transitional period – indeed, took an active part in it through his leadership role in the Italian Communist Party – explains the ambiguous and seemingly contradictory nature of some aspects of his theory. On the one hand, Gramsci was one of the first Marxists to articulate fresh concepts and insights on the basis of anticipated fundamental changes within bourgeois society itself; on the other, he remained situated in an historical period dominated by the Bolshevik Revolution and the Comintern, the failure of socialist uprisings in the West, and the rise of fascism and Stalinism. Disenchanted with the mechanical Marxism of Social Democracy, Gramsci instinctively looked to the Leninist model as a source of inspiration and strategy. Then, with the consolidation of capitalism in Europe and the triumph of bureaucratic centralism in the Soviet Union, he began to work out some theoretical alternatives – though, *politically* speaking, he continued to take for granted most of the original Bolshevik premises. It is therefore no wonder that, aside from the obstacles imposed by years of prison confinement, Gramsci could not fully explore and develop the implications of his own thought for the tasks of revolutionary politics in the advanced capitalist systems.

Yet the implications are there, for those who are interested in advancing contemporary Marxist theory and practice on the basis of past contributions. Gramsci, of course, cannot supply the concrete historical understanding necessary to build a revolutionary movement in present conditions; but his theoretical-strategic framework does contain, in its most universalistic aspect, concepts and principles that make intelligible the new modes of rebellion in advanced capitalism and suggest a particular direction of political struggle for the future.

In the *Prison Notebooks*, Gramsci had predicted that the growing complexity of civil society in the most advanced capitalist countries would raise ideological-cultural struggle to a new level, since the state would increasingly rest its authority upon hegemony rather than force. The old dichotomy between base and superstructure, state and civil society would gradually be dissolved into a broad 'ensemble of relations', rendering the revolutionary process more totalistic and multi-dimensional, and undermining the catastrophist approach that relied upon crisis and seizure of state power as the mechanism of the transition to socialism. What Gramsci foresaw in the 1930s was perhaps nowhere more fully realized than in the United States after the end of the Second World War, though the main tendencies are clearly visible elsewhere – in Western Europe, Canada, and Japan. Modern bourgeois society includes just about everything Gramsci had in mind, and more: diversification of the proletariat, the technological revolution, and with it the rapidly-expanded role of science and education in production, the penetration throughout civil society of bureaucratic norms of authority and work, the rise of mass media and communications and the diffusion of popular culture, the breakdown of the distinction between public and private realms of existence. Hegemonic values and behaviour patterns extend throughout every sphere of civil society – schools, the media, culture, trade unions, the family, as well as the workplace – and become interwoven into the structural and ideological totality of capitalism. The socialization process through which people internalize these dominant values, and the alienation that results from it, is no less universal. In comparison with previous class systems, including the earlier stages of competitive capitalism, the ideological resources available to the modern-day ruling class would seem to present massive obstacles to any revolutionary movement. The 'one-dimensionality' of advanced technocratic capitalism is unquestionably a compelling force; yet the very totalization of bourgeois hegemony creates new opportunities for subversive opposition, and in many ways renders the system more vulnerable than ever.

What Gramsci anticipated, and what has become the reality of contemporary capitalism, is the importance of the struggle for ideological hegemony as the precondition for socialist transformation – a problematic quite different from that formulated by either classical Marxism or Leninism, or confronted by Third World liberation movements today. It is the problematic of building a new collective consciousness by attacking, through ideological-cultural struggle and political action, all of the 'intellectual-moral' foundations of bourgeois society. This means precisely what the American new left groped for in practice but what it never understood as part of any long-range political strategy: a thoroughgoing cultural revolution that sets out to transform all dimensions of everyday life and establish the social-psychological underpinnings of socialism *before* the question of organized state power is resolved. As Franz Schurmann has observed:

> Revolutions do not begin with the thunderclap of a seizure of power – that is their culmination. They start with attacks on the moral-political order and the traditional hierarchy of class statuses. They succeed when the power structure, beset by its own irresolvable contradictions, can no longer perform legitimately and effectively. It is often forgotten that the state has often in the past been rescued by the moral-political order and the class hierarchy (authority) that the people still accepted.[2]

To the extent that the universalization of different forms of ideological hegemony in advanced capitalism accelerates this dynamic, the old strategic solutions – economism, spontaneist anarchism and Leninism – appear increasingly anachronistic in their narrow partiality. What the Gramscian approach encompasses is a 'dialectics of consciousness' that is rooted in the 'phenomenology of everyday life'.[3]

The various aspects of ideological hegemony – whatever their different histories and peculiar dynamics, whatever their relationship (past or present) to given structures, whatever their origins in a particular kind of oppression – constitute at the same time the *totality* of bourgeois hegemony in contemporary capitalist society. Each dominant system of beliefs has its specific quality, yet all are intertwined to such an extent that this totality is bound to permeate most concrete institutions, situations, events, personalities, and even the oppositional movements themselves. With the increasing complexity of civil society and its interpenetration with the state, the attempt to abstract and isolate particular elements from the larger whole – what Gramsci called the 'ensemble of relations' – becomes more and more hopeless. The subversive attack against one area of hegemony must therefore, at some point, move to the level of totality that incorporates a broader struggle against all the dominant ideologies that support oppressive structures. All areas of hegemony function together, with varying impact and emphasis from one context to another, to produce and reify a generalized alienation that results in passivity, a sense of powerlessness, subcultural fragmentation, separation of the personal and political, etc. Sense of community in any truly public or liberating form is consistently denied by the reproduction of bourgeois hegemony in peoples' everyday lives, from the family to the workplace and neighbourhoods. Since, as Gramsci emphasized, the oppressed must demystify the ideological armour of the status quo and create their own 'integrated culture' prior to and within the process of achieving economic and political control, it follows that destroying this hegemonic totality must be central to the calculations of any revolutionary movement.

To combat this universalized hegemony means to transform repressive consciousness into a liberating one that makes socialist politics at a *mass* level possible – the central focus of any thoroughgoing cultural revolution. It is a task much more complex and multidimensional than anything defined by classical Marxism or Leninism, or even by the 'underground' tradition, given the limitations of its historical situation. One of the first priorities of such a cultural revolution is to transform the character structure and personal existence that is the mechanism of repressive consiousness in a way that, as Paulo Freire suggests, people in their everyday lives can 'discover' the oppressor in their own minds and struggle to become the self-affirming subjects of their own destiny, capable of 'seeing a new world through new eyes'.[4] Since every hegemonic world-view is so deeply-imbued in the individual consciousness, ideological struggle must above all confront the most concrete issues of personal and social existence – what Marxists have previously dismissed as 'trivial' or 'subjective'. Freire refers to the idea of building around a complex of themes – the 'thematic universe' – rooted in a particular community; only once the old ways of thinking and behaving come under serious challenge, when the time-honoured myths, fears, and superstitions have been dispelled, does a critical consciousness become possible[5]. And once one realm of the 'thematic universe' starts to crumble, the remainder might begin to disintegrate too, depending upon historical conditions. Because a major function of ideological hegemony is to repress popular feelings of anger, resentment, and frustration or contain them to the individual sphere, this dialectic of politicizing the personal concerns of everyday life is strategically central.

But this project stands little chance of realization if one of the hallmarks of the English-speaking left – hostility to theory – is not at some point overcome. 'Theory' is all too often *opposed* to politics, to practice, to everyday life, as something intrinsically outside the revolutionary process, just as in an obverse way 'action' (of whatever sort) has been glorified as an end in itself. It is true that such notions are often motivated by a concern that is anything but revolutionary – whether reformist, spontaneist, disengaged, or even apathetic – but what is astonishing is the rejection of theory within a political community that has claimed to be anti-capitalist, socialist, radical, etc. That these tendencies should be so strong in societies with unprecedented educational and intellectual resources is even more ironic. The fact that theory was never alien (indeed was integral) to the great revolutions of the twentieth century has never been internalized or even appreciated by the English-speaking left. 'Theory' has been associated with the obscurantism and dilettantism of the academic elites, and nothing more; it has rarely been seen as a guide to revolutionary action, as an inseparable element of *praxis*.

Those who spurn theory in favour of concrete activities of the moment not only do a great disservice to the basic Marxist conception of the unity of theory and practice, but inevitably wind up avoiding the really complex issues and dilemmas the left must resolve if it is to make real progress. In this sense theory is nothing other than the cognitive dimension of revolution – thinking seriously and systematically about the goals, methods, strategies, and tactics of revolutionary politics. Many different intellectual activities can contribute to this task, of course, but the point is that the two realms of theory and practice, thought and action must be brought together, not separated; the one-sided embracing of one or the other reduces both of them to undialectical, empty abstractions – at least as far as socialist revolution is concerned. In particular, the obsession with immediate practical solutions, with concrete choices, with 'getting things done' (so central to the whole American tradition of pragmatism and anti-intellectualism) can only work *through*, and not *against*, the dominant bourgeois categories of thought and action. It can never challenge, transcend, or overturn them, no matter how militant and courageous it might be. In Gramscian terms, *the action-oriented politics or pragmatism can only reproduce bourgeois ideological hegemony. Thus 'no theory' is really, in the final analysis, nothing other than bourgeois ideology.* The role of revolutionary theory is to create the foundation of a new socialist order precisely through the negation and transendence of bourgeois society; there is no strictly 'pragmatic' or instrumental solution to this task, insofar as it depends upon the development of a qualitatively new *Weltanschauung* and culture.

At the same time, much more than 'theory' in the traditional sense is needed to shape political practice. Gramsci's thought opens up an entirely new approach to revolution – one that introduces a new conception of theory itself in the total transformative process. By Gramsci's definition, all human beings are in a fundamental sense philosophers and intellectuals (i.e. 'theorists') in that they are thinking, creative, social beings who can readily participate in the world-historical process of building a new culture. To the extent that everyone has beliefs, ideas, feelings, aesthetics as they participate in an evolving social and cultural order, to the extent that everyone exercises a certain impact upon their surroundings, everyone is potentially a theorist, a bearer of consciousness. Of course other questions remain: the nature and level of consciousness, the particular role and contribution of a given agent, the effectiveness in transmitting values, etc. But Gramsci's vision opens up the prospects of 'democratizing' theory by breaking down within a revolutionary movement the historic division of labour between intellectuals and masses, experts and laymen, elites and followers This means eliminating, eventually, the split between mental and physical forms of activity that is so central to the social division of labour in bourgeois society itself. It follows that theory in the *revolutionary* sense can no longer be 'autonomous' (on whatever grounds) but can only become viable as an organic part of the struggle to transform everyday life. The repository of Marxism cannot be an organized vanguard or intellectual *elite*; it must be the oppressed strata themselves.

Historically, much of the European Marxist tradition (often

conceived of as 'science', or some kind of esoteric body of knowledge) has been unnecessarily remote to all but a very small nucleus of high-powered theorists. Perhaps this was an historically-necessary stage. Yet within the American left, say, Marxism has all too often been manipulated for elitist and opportunistic purposes – which helps to explain the contemporary popular revulsion against theory of any sort. Gramsci insisted, however, that what distinguished Marxism from past theories and philosophical systems was that it was the first authentically *popular* theory; it was not enough for revolutionaries to write sophisticated philosophical treatises and elaborate analyses of capitalism and imperialism, though these would be surely indispensable. What for Gramsci was more crucial in the long run was the mass diffusion of a socialist world-view – including a broadly critical understanding of the existing society, a vision of the future, and a strategic sense of how to get there. Gramsci sought to incorporate theory into a new popular language, which is where the linkage between politics and philosophy is ultimately grounded.

References

Introduction / pp.11–20

1. The initial Italian publications of Gramsci's prison writings (*Quaderni del Carcere*) were assembled by Einaudi in six volumes between 1948 and 1951. An anthology of Gramsci's writings, edited by Mario Spinella and Carlo Salinari, was published by Editori Riuniti in 1963. Recently the most significant of Gramsci's writings on politics and philosophy have been translated into English and brought together into an excellent volume. See Quintin Hoare and Geoffrey Nowell-Smith, eds, *Selections from the Prison Notebooks of Antonio Gramsci* (London: Lawrence and Wishart 1971). Most of the citations from Gramsci's prison writings in this book are from this volume. For writings between 1915 and 1926, the main source has been Paolo Spriano, ed, *Antonio Gramsci: Scritti Politici* (Roma: Editori Riuniti, 1967), an exhaustive collection that contains the bulk of Gramsci's pre-prison articles in *Avanti!*, *Il Grido del Popolo*, *L'Ordine Nuovo*, *L'Unità*, and *Stato Operaio*, as well as his contributions to official party (mainly PCI) literature. Little of Gramsci's early writings has been translated into English; there is only a scattered collection of *Ordine Nuovo* articles from the 1919–1920 period brought together under the heading 'Soviets in Italy' in *New Left Review* no.51 (1968).
2. Giuseppi Fiori, *Antonio Gramsci: Life of a Revolutionary* (London: New Left Books 1970 and New York: E.P.Dutton and Co 1971), p.237.
3. 'Letter to Tatiana', 15 December 1930, in Lynne Lawner, ed, *Letters from Prison by Antonio Gramsci* (New York: Harper and Row 1973), p.193.

1. Marxism as the 'Philosophy of Praxis' / pp.21–35

1. 'The Study of Philosophy', in Hoare and Nowell-Smith, eds, *Selections from The Prison Notebooks of Antonio Gramsci*, p.336.
2. 'Tre principi, tre ordini' and 'Margini', both from *La Città Futura*, in Spriano, ed, *Scritti Politici*, pp.42–46 and 53.
3. 'La Rivoluzione contro il "Capitale"', *Avanti!* (24 November 1918), in *Scritti Politici*, pp.80–83.
4. 'Problems of Marxism', *Prison Notebooks*, p.429.
5. *ibid*.

6. In actuality, Gramsci did not think it would be possible to construct a Marxism that would even approach the precision of the natural sciences, and he found rather amusing the efforts of theorists like Bukharin to do so. Typical of many quotations found throughout the *Prison Notebooks* is the following: 'The so-called laws of sociology which are assumed as laws of causation have no causal value: they are almost always tautologies and paralogisms. Usually they are no more than a duplicate of the observed fact itself. The only novelty is the collective name given to a series of petty facts.' 'Problems of Marxism', *Prison Notebooks*, p.430.

7. See Karl Korsch, *Marxism and Philosophy* (London: New Left Books and New York: Monthly Review Press 1970). In Korsch's words: 'To accord theory an autonomous existence outside of the objective movement of history would obviously be neither materialist, nor dialectical in the Hegelian sense; it would simply be an idealist metaphysic.' (p.58.) He continues: 'For example, many bourgeois interpreters of Marx and some later Marxists thought they were able to distinguish between the historical and the theoretico-economic material in Marx's major work *Capital*; but all they proved by this is that they understood nothing of the real method of Marx's critique of political economy. For it is one of the essential signs of his dialectical materialist method that this distinction does not exist for it; it is indeed precisely a theoretical comprehension of history.' (p.59.) This was written in 1923; though it is not clear exactly how much influence Korsch had upon Gramsci's philosophical formulations in the *Prison Notebooks*, their positions are remarkably similar.

8. 'Theses on Feuerbach', in *Karl Marx and Frederick Engels: Selected Works* (New York: International Publishers 1968), p.28.

9. 'The Study of Philosophy', *Prison Notebooks*, p.353. (Italics in the original.)

10. 'Problems of Marxism', *Prison Notebooks*, p.465. Elsewhere Gramsci writes about the 'subjective universal', and 'objectivity that is part of man and being'. Thus, 'We know reality only in relation to man, and since man is historical becoming, knowledge and reality are also a becoming and so is objectivity, etc.' ('Problems of Marxism', *Prison Notebooks*, p.446).

11. *ibid.*, pp.437–438.

12. 'The Modern Prince', *Prison Notebooks*, p.171. Gramsci goes on to expand on this theme: 'It is certain that prediction only means seeing the present and the past clearly as movement. Seeing them clearly: in other words, accurately identifying the fundamental and permanent elements of the process. But it is absurd to think of a purely "objective" prediction. Anybody who makes a prediction has in fact a "programme" for whose victory he is working, and his prediction is precisely an element contributing to that victory.' *ibid.*

13. 'The Study of Philosophy', *Prison Notebooks*, p.372.
14. 'The Study of Philosophy', *Prison Notebooks*, p.360. In another section of the *Prison Notebooks* Gramsci makes this point in a somewhat less Hegelian manner: 'If it is true that man cannot be conceived of except as historically-determined man – i.e. man who has developed, and who lives, in certain conditions, in a particular social complex or totality of social relations – is it then possible to take sociology as meaning simply the study of these conditions and the laws which regulate their development? Since the will and initiative of men themselves cannot be left out of account, this notion must be false. The problem of what "science" itself is has to be posed. Is not science itself "political activity" and "political thought", inasmuch as it transforms men and makes them different from what they were before?' 'State and Civil Society', *Prison Notebooks*, p.244.
15. 'The Study of Philosophy', *Prison Notebooks*, p.367.
16. 'Problems of Marxism', *Prison Notebooks*, p.470.
17. *ibid.* p.392.
18. 'The Study of Philosophy', *Prison Notebooks*, p.326.
19. Gramsci's conception of a critical Marxism, though nowhere explicitly defined as such in the *Prison Notebooks*, would seem to converge at points with the 'critical theory' developed at about the same time by Max Horkheimer, Herbert Marcuse, and the Frankfurt School tradition in Germany and the United States. But there are some crucial differences, notably in the much closer linkage between philosophy and politics (in both theory *and* practice) that one finds in Gramsci. For an excellent general discussion of the rise of critical theory, see Martin Jay, *The Dialectical Imagination: The Frankfurt School and the Rise of Critical Theory*, 1930–1950 (Boston: Little, Brown Co 1973), ch. 2.
20. 'The Study of Philosophy', *Prison Notebooks*, p.325.
21. *ibid.* pp.332–333.
22. Here again, Gramsci's position closely resembles that of Korsch. Cf. *Marxism and Philosophy*, pp.75–81.
23. 'Letter to Tatiana' [Gramsci's sister-in-law], 9 May 1932, in Lawner, *op. cit.*, pp.236–237. On one occasion Gramsci referred to Croce as the 'high priest of contemporary historicist religion'.
24. See, for example, Carlo Marzani, *The Open Marxism of Antonio Gramsci* (New York: Cameron Associates 1957), introduction; Gwyn

Williams, 'Gramsci's concept of Egemonia', *Journal of the History of Ideas* (October–December, 1960); Eugene Genovese, 'On Antonio Gramsci', *Studies on the Left* (March–April 1967); and H. Stuart Hughes, *Consciousness and Society* (New York: Vintage Books 1958), epilogue to ch. 5. An excellent critique of the tendency to evaluate Gramsci's Marxism in strictly idealist terms is the introduction by Carlo Salinari and Mario Spinella to the Italian anthology of Gramsci's writings. See *Antonio Gramsci: Antologia degli Scritti* (Roma: Editori Riuniti 1963).

25. 'Problems of Marxism', *Prison Notebooks*, pp.404–405.
26. *ibid.* p.462.

2. Ideological Hegemony and Class Struggle / pp.36–54

1. 'Problems of Marxism', *Prison Notebooks*, p.407. This premise was also accepted by Lenin and Mao tse-Tung, though neither dealt with the problem as extensively as did Gramsci.
2. 'The Study of Philosophy', *Prison Notebooks*, p.377.
3. Thus, Gramsci states that 'the general notion of the state includes elements which need to be referred back to the notion of civil society (in the sense that one might say that State = political society + civil society, in other words hegemony protected by the armour of coercion).' 'State and Civil Society', *Prison Notebooks*, p.263. The thrust of Gramsci's conceptual contribution to the Marxist theory of state is weakened here, however, by his failure to clearly specify the boundaries between political society and civil society. For example, modern-day political parties and interest groups would not appear to belong exclusively to either category.
4. 'Notes on Italian History', *Prison Notebooks*, pp.103–104. For an excellent general treatment of Gramsci's concept of hegemony in English, see John M. Cammett, *Antonio Gramsci and the Origins of Italian Communism* (Stanford, Calif.: Stanford University Press 1967), ch. 10.
5. 'State and Civil Society', *Prison Notebooks*, p.270.
6. 'The Modern Prince', *Prison Notebooks*, p.210. Gramsci actually refers to this situation as a 'crisis of authority' which can be resolved either in the direction of reaction ('Caesarism') or revolution, depending upon the level of ideological preparation of the left itself as well as any number of 'imponderable factors' (which recalls Machiavelli's notion of *fortuna*).
7. 'State and Civil Society', *Prison Notebooks*, p.276.
8. On the role of Croce, Gramsci wrote that 'it is precisely in civil society that intellectuals operate especially (Benedetto Croce, for example, is a kind of lay

pope and an extremely efficient instrument of hegemony – even if at times he may find himself in disagreement with one government or another).' 'Notes on Italian History', *Prison Notebooks*, p.56.

9. 'Americanism and Fordism', *Prison Notebooks*, esp. pp.300–305.

10. *ibid.* p.300, pp.304–305.

11. For an interesting comparison of Gramsci and Marcuse, see Alastair Davidson, *Antonio Gramsci: The Man, His Ideas* (Sydney: Australian Left Review Publications, 1969), ch. 4.

12. 'Americanism and Fordism', pp.304–305.

13. 'State and Civil Society', *Prison Notebooks*, p.238. Or, as Gramsci writes in a more strategic vein: 'The massive structures of the modern democracies, both as State organizations, and as complexes of organizations in civil society, constitute for the art of politics as it were the "trenches" and the permanent fortifications of the front in the war of position; they render merely "partial" the element of movement which before used to be "the whole" of war, etc.' *ibid.* p.243.

14. 'The Modern Prince', *Prison Notebooks*, p.188.

15. The best historical treatment of these phenomena in the *Prison Notebooks* is in 'Problems of Marxism', *Prison Notebooks*, pp.393–399. Needless to say, the examples discussed here pose a number of dilemmas for Marxism itself, of which Gramsci was acutely aware. As Gramsci put it, one theoretical contribution of Marxism was the dynamic interrelationship between leaders and masses that it specified. But the historical predicament of Marxism was that in practice 'the great intellectuals formed on the terrain of this philosophy, besides being few in number, were not linked with the people, they did not emerge from the people, but were the expression of traditional intermediary classes, to which they returned at the great 'turning points' of history.' *ibid.* p.397.

16. 'Notes on Italian History', *Prison Notebooks*, p.106.

17. The general outline of Gramsci's analysis here is contained in fragments spread throughout his 'Notes on Italian History'. Its relevance to political strategy will be taken up in Chapter 5.

18. 'Americanism and Fordism', *Prison Notebooks*, p.285.

19. 'The Intellectuals', *Prison Notebooks*, p.20.

20. Gramsci's analysis of American development here bears a close resemblance to the later interpretation advanced by Louis Hartz in his *Liberal Tradition in America* (New York: Harcourt, Brace, and World 1955) and *The Founding of New Societies* (New York: Harcourt, Brace, and World 1964), introduction and ch. 1. Gramsci's treatment, based as it was

upon inadequate historical sources, was much more fragmentary and lacked the depth Hartz's account possessed. It also revealed a weak grasp of the importance of slavery and black history, an understable omission but one that weakens some of the general propositions nonetheless. Yet when one examines the problem from a comparative perspective, Gramsci's insights are still highly impressive for their richness and originality.

21. 'Notes on Italian History', *Prison Notebooks*, p.57.
22. 'State and Civil Society', *Prison Notebooks*, p.235.

3. Mass Consciousness and Revolution / pp.55–84

1. Wilhelm Reich, 'What is Class Consciousness', in Lee Baxandall, ed, *Sex-Pol: Essays, 1929–1934* (New York: Vintage Books 1972), p.284.
2. *ibid.*, pp.288–289.
3. *ibid.*, pp.290–291. On the issue of ideology itself, Reich says that 'Any revolutionary who underestimates the material power of ideology is certain to fail. In our period of history, it has proved stronger than the power of material poverty; were this not so, the working class, not Hitler and Thyssen, would be in power today.' *ibid.*, p.310.
4. This quotation is from an article that Gramsci wrote for the socialist newspaper *Il Grido* in the spring of 1916, and is taken from Fiori, *op. cit.*, p.103.
5. For an extensive account of Gramsci's critique of the PSI, see Cammett, *op. cit.*, chs. 3 and 4.
6. The bulk of Gramsci's writings between 1921 and 1926 take up this theme of the decline of established Marxist parties (manifest in their failure to act decisively to further socialist objectives) in the context of Mussolini's rise to power. See in particular 'Problemi morali e lotta de classe', *L'Ordine Nuovo* (7 August 1921), in *Scritti Politici*, pp.469–471; 'I Partiti e la massa', *L'Ordine Nuovo* (25 September 1921), in *ibid.*, pp.492–495; and 'La Funzione del riformismo in Italia', *L'Unità* (5 February 1925), in *ibid.*, pp.591–594.
7. 'Marinetti Rivoluzionario?', *L'Ordine Nuovo* (5 January 1921), in *Scritti Politici*, pp.413–414.
8. Letter to Tatiana (19 November 1928), in Lawner, *op. cit.*, p.136.
9. 'The Modern Prince', *Prison Notebooks*, p.184.
10. Gramsci himself never entertained Sorel's conception of the General Strike, but he did recognize Sorel as one of the few creative theorists on the European left. The relationship between the two was close for a time during Gramsci's *Ordine Nuovo* period, in part because of the 'syndicalist' orienta-

tion they shared, but major differences became increasingly apparent as Sorel's thought took a romanticist turn that eventually gave support to a militant anti-Marxism. The influence of Sorel's ideas on the Gramsci of the *Prison Notebooks* was therefore remote and quite limited, although a reading of *Reflections on Violence* reveals a number of striking similarities.

11. Quoted from 'Notes on Machiavelli', *Prison Notebooks*, p.187.

12. 'State and Civil Society', *Prison Notebooks*, p.187.

13. For an analysis of 'primitive' or 'pre-political' types of rebellion in Italy (and elsewhere), see E.J.Hobsbawm, *Primitive Rebels* (New York: W.W.Norton and Company, 1959).

14. 'Problems of Marxism', *Prison Notebooks*, p.421. At another point in his critique Gramsci pokes fun at Bukharin's preoccupation with the 'great philosophical and scientific systems' to the exclusion of the real problem of mass consciousness: 'Reading the *Manual* one has the impression of someone who cannot sleep for the moonlight and who struggles to massacre the fireflies in the belief that by so doing he will make the brightness lessen or disappear.' 'Problems of Marxism', p.433.

15. Rosa Luxemburg, 'Mass Strike, Party, and Trade Unions', in Dick Howard, ed, *Selected Political Writings of Rosa Luxemburg* (New York: Monthly Review Press 1971), p.201.

16. Luxemburg, 'The Organizational Questions of Russian Social Democracy', in *ibid.*, p.288.

17. Georg Lukacs, *History and Class Consciousness*, translated by Rodney Livingstone. (London: Merlin Press and Cambridge, Mass: MIT Press 1971), p.20.

18. *ibid.*, p.22. In a typical passage, Lukacs wrote that 'Consciousness does not lie outside the real process of history. It does not have to be introduced into the world by philosophers.' (p.77.) Much later, in his own introduction to *History and Class Consciousness*, Lukacs would criticize his conception of an 'imputed' consciousness that could never supply the foundations of a revolutionary praxis.

19. Andrew Arato, 'Lukacs: in Search of the Revolutionary Subject', in Klare and Howard, eds, *op. cit.*, p.101.

20. For an excellent discussion of the relationship between spontaneism and Jacobinism in the Marxist tradition, although more explicitly in reference to the role of the party, see Lucio Magri, 'Problems of the Marxist Theory of the Revolutionary Party', *New Left Review* no.60.

21. As early as 1918, however, Gramsci was praising Lenin's 'creative' approach to revolution and cited the Bolshevik success as a possible model. See

'L'Opera di Lenin', from *Il Grido del Popolo* (14 September 1918), in *Scritti Politici*, p.163. At about the same time Gramsci had also begun to move toward his own critique of spontaneism, for example in his 'Cultura e lotta di classe', from *Il Grido del Popolo* (25 May 1918), in *ibid.*, pp.137–139.

22. These general criticisms of the spontaneist position have a basis in Gramsci's overall theory rather than in any specific attacks on Luxemburg and Lukacs. Although there are scattered references to Luxemburg throughout the *Prison Notebooks*, most of them are in fact favourable and nowhere does Gramsci really discuss her theory of consciousness. He did, however, briefly criticize her notion of 'crisis' set forth in *The Mass Strike*, as follows: 'It was thus out and out historical mysticism, the awaiting of a sort of miraculous illumination.' ('State and Civil Society', *Prison Notebooks*, p.233.) As for Lukacs, there is only one mention of his thought in the *Prison Notebooks*, and that is a very brief critique of the dialectic in Lukacs's work that appears to stem from a misunderstanding of Lukacs's application of the dialectic in *History and Class Consciousness*.

For a very summary critique of Lukacs from a Gramscian perspective, see Magri, *op. cit.*, pp.111–113. This article represents a refreshing departure from the normal tendency to lump together Gramsci and Lukacs as postwar exponents of 'Hegelianized' Marxism (with the usual charges of 'historicism', 'voluntarism', 'idealism', etc.). Certainly the Hegelian influence upon both theorists is very strong, particularly in their methodological attack on positivism, but their concrete formulations of critical problems differ so greatly that it is amazing they have been identified by the same label for so long.

An excellent and more extensive critical analysis of Lukacs' thought can be found in Gareth Stedman-Jones, 'The Marxism of the Early Lukacs: an Evaluation', *New Left Review* no.70.

23. 'Problems of Marxism', *Prison Notebooks*, p.422.

24. 'La Volontà delle masse', *L'Unità* (24 June 1925), in *Scritti Politici*, pp.620–621.

25. 'Problems of Marxism', *Prison Notebooks*, p.423.

26. The difficulty here is of course enormous, as Gramsci realized: 'The principle elements of common sense are provided by religion, and consequently the relationship between common sense and religion is much more intimate than that between common sense and the philosophical systems of the intellectuals [e.g. Marxism].' 'Problems of Marxism', p.420. In pointing to religion Gramsci of course had in mind the uniquely powerful role of the Catholic Church in Italy.

27. 'The Modern Prince', *Prison Notebooks*, pp.192–193.
28. *ibid.*, p.199.
29. 'State and Civil Society', *Prison Notebooks*, pp.272–273. Gramsci's distinction between 'generic' or 'semi-feudal' and 'modern' forms of revolt parallels Hobsbawm's distinction between 'primitive' and 'modern' rebellion – the former chaotic and 'pre-political', the latter possessing coherent theory and ideology, leadership and organization, and a particular 'target' e.g. the state). See Hobsbawm, *passim.*
30. 'The Modern Prince', *Prison Notebooks*, pp.181–182. By 'fundamental social group' Gramsci meant 'class', while, presumably, 'subordinate groups' here refer to what might be called 'interest groups'.

   In defining revolutionary consciousness at another point, Gramsci wrote: 'The concept of revolutionary and of internationalist, in the modern sense of the word, is correlative with the precise concept of state and of class: little understanding of the state means little class consciousness (and understanding of the state exists not only when one defends it, but also when one attacks it in order to overthrow it . . .)' 'State and Civil Society', *Prison Notebooks*, p.275.
31. 'The Modern Prince', *Prison Notebooks*, p.201.
32. *ibid.*, p.198.
33. 'The Intellectuals', *Prison Notebooks*, p.9. Also: 'the majority of mankind are philosophers insofar as they engage in practical activity and in their practical activity (or in their guiding lines of conduct) there is implicitly contained a conception of the world, a philosophy.' 'The Study of Philosophy', *Prison Notebooks*, p.344.
34. 'The Intellectuals', *Prison Notebooks*, p.10. In addition, the intellectual function for Gramsci involved both the *diffusion* and the creating of ideas – most importantly the former: 'Creating a new culture does not only mean one's own individual "original" discoveries. It also, and most particularly, means the diffusion in a critical form of truths already discovered, their "socialization", as it were, and even making them the basis of vital action, an element of co-ordination and intellectual and moral order.' 'The Study of Philosophy', *Prison Notebooks*, p.325.
35. 'The Study of Philosophy', *Prison Notebooks*, p.339.
36. 'The Intellectuals', *Prison Notebooks*, p.10. Gramsci also introduced the notion of 'democratic philosopher' – 'the historical realization of a new type of philosopher . . . in the sense that he is a philosopher convinced that his personality . . . is an active social relationship of modification of the cultural environment.' 'The Study of Philosophy', *Prison Notebooks*, p.350.

37. Gramsci was very aware of the hidden dangers in this strategic approach. One such danger might be the tendency to view political struggle in intellectualistic terms, i.e. to see it as simply consciousness transformation without considering the imperatives of the state and political power. Another might be the development of fatalistic or indifferent attitudes towards the revolutionary process, given the necessarily long-range, organic nature of change Gramsci had in mind. The priority of building a stratum of 'organic' intellectuals could be invoked to avoid the dictates of conscious intervention. This is perhaps why Gramsci so harshly attacked Croce's brand of historicism (isolating the 'ethical' moment) which he argued could lead only to 'political morphinism'. See 'Notes on Italian history', *Prison Notebooks*, p.114.

38. 'Problems of Marxism', *Prison Notebooks*, p.417.

39. *ibid.*, p.418.

40. On this point, see Lucio Colletti, 'Gramsci and Revolution', *New Left Review* no.65. This type of 'frontism' should not be confused with the United Front approach earlier adopted by the Communist International – a tactic that sought to advance socialism as an immediate goal by unifying the working class around a common anti-capitalist programme.

41. This analysis of the transformation of the PCI in postwar Italy is close to the one advanced by the *Il Manifesto* group, which originated in 1969 within the PCI and was later expelled. The influence of Gramsci's thought upon this movement is evident both in its general strategy for socialist revolution (e.g. emphasis upon transforming mass consciousness, the role of extra-parliamentary struggle) and in its particular inclination towards soviets. For an excellent treatment of the postwar PCI by one of the leading *Il Manifesto* intellectuals, see Lucio Magri, 'Italian Communism in the Sixties', *New Left Review* no.66.

42. 'The Study of Philosophy', *Prison Notebooks*, p.366, 377.

43. Gramsci's strategy of a 'national-popular' alliance of Northern workers and Southern peasants, which differed somewhat from Lenin's conception of peasants as an 'auxiliary force', was an outgrowth of his interest in 'the problem of the *Mezzogiorno*' and his understanding of the regional peculiarities of Italian development. At the same time, Gramsci was acutely aware of the dangers inherent in such an alliance – not to mention the notion of the 'historical bloc' itself – since a multiplicity of forces might bring into a movement diverse priorities and interests that could create a situation of immobilizing conflict or a compromise policy of partial reforms. A movement or party based on such a fragile 'bloc' would, according to Gramsci, in any case disintegrate at a moment of crisis when 'fundamental' issues come into play. See 'The Modern Prince', *Prison Notebooks*, pp.157–158.

4. The Factory Councils: Nucleus of the 'New State' / pp.85–100

1. Though Gramsci nowhere developed the theme of prefigurative struggle in the *Prison Notebooks* (it is the product of his *Ordine Nuovo* theorizing), his sensitivity to it is revealed there from time to time. See, for example, 'State and Civil Society', *Prison Notebooks*, pp.264–265 and 268–269. Gramsci's later preoccupation with the role of the party and his failure to develop further the idea of the workers' councils and soviets can be explained by several factors: (1) his attempt to correct the earlier imbalance that seemed at times to dwell exclusively on the councils; (2) a sense that he had explored the topic adequately in the *Ordine Nuovo* period and that he now wanted to devote his limited energy to other problems; and (3) his growing concern over fascism and the means whereby the Italian left might succeed in averting destruction. It is true that Gramsci became more critical of the Turin council movement after 1922, but never to the extent of rejecting its fundamental premises. Still, it is too bad that Gramsci never really took up the problem of the councils in the *Notebooks* (especially in its relationship to the role of the party), since it leaves some important strategic questions unanswered.

2. 'Le Masse e i capi', *L'Ordine Nuovo* (30 October 1921), in *Scritti Politici*, p.501.

3. 'Sindacati e consigli', *L'Ordine Nuovo* (12 June 1920), in *Scritti Politici*, p.341.

4. 'Sindacato e consigli', *L'Ordine Nuovo* (11 October 1919), in *Scritti Politici*, p.248.

5. *ibid.*, p.246.

6. 'Per un rinnovamento del Partito socialista', *L'Ordine Nuovo* (8 May 1920), in *Scritti Politici*, p.319.

7. *ibid.*, p.320.

8. 'Il Partito comunista', *L'Ordine Nuovo* (9 October 1920), in *Scritti Politici*, p.365.

9. *L'Ordine Nuovo* reached an average of 5,000 subscribers, a majority of them workers in the Turin area, during the 1919–1921 period. Gramsci and the other Marxist intellectuals of the council movement did not publish *L'Ordine Nuovo* as theorists detached from the everyday life of the workers but as

political activists helping the workers to understand their situation in a theoretical way. Gramsci wrote that: 'I, Togliatti, and Terracini were invited to hold debates in educational institutes and factory assemblies; the shop committees invited us to small group discussions... The development of the shop committees became the central problem, indeed the *idea* behind the *Ordine Nuovo*: the fundamental problem of a working-class revolution, the problem of "liberty" for workers. *Ordine Nuovo* became for us and our supporters the "newspaper" of the factory councils.' From *L'Ordine Nuovo* (14 August 1920), quoted in Lynne Lawner, ed, *The Prison Letters of Antonio Gramsci*, pp.138–139.

10. 'La Conquista dello stato', *L'Ordine Nuovo* (12 July 1919), in *Scritti Politici*, p.221.

11. 'Il Consiglio di fabbrica', *L'Ordine Nuovo* (5 June 1920), in *Scritti Politici*, p.334. In a passage from the same article, Gramsci wrote that the revolutionary process unfolds 'subterraneously, in the darkness of the factory and in the obscurity of the consciousness of the countless multitudes that capitalism subjects to its laws', *ibid*.

12. 'Sindacato e consigli', *L'Ordine Nuovo* (11 October 1919), in *Scritti Politici*, p.248.

13. 'Sindacati e consigli', *L'Ordine Nuovo* (12 June 1920), in *Scritti Politici*, p.340.

14. Il consiglio di fabbrica', *L'Ordine Nuovo* (5 June 1920), in *Scritti Politici*, p.336.

15. See, for example, 'Controllo operaio', *L'Ordine Nuovo* (10 February 1921), in *Scritti Politici*, pp. 411–412.

16. 'Il Partito e la rivoluzione', *L'Ordine Nuovo* (27 December 1919), in *Scritti Politici*, p.292.

17. One fairly comprehensive pre-prison critique of the council movement is Gramsci's 'Ancora della capacità organische della classe operaia', *L'Unità* (1 October 1926), in *Scritti Politici*, pp.705–707.

5. The Revolutionary Party / pp.101–118

1. See in particular Sheldon Wolin, *Politics and Vision* (New York: Little, Brown, and Company 1961), ch. 9.

2. Stanley Moore, *Three Tactics: The Background in Marx* (New York: Monthly Review Press 1963). Moore distinguishes among 'minority revolution' (Lenin), 'majority revolution' (Kautsky), and 'reformism' (Bernstein) as types of Marxist strategy. Some have argued that it is impossible to identify any single 'Leninism', since Lenin himself changed theoretical and tactical positions in his own writings in response to different situations and events. That Lenin was very changeable on some questions and even inconsistent is beyond doubt; yet, at the most general political level, what emerges out of the theory and practice of the Bolsheviks under Lenin's guidance – from the RSDLP split in 1903, to the struggle with the Mensheviks, to the October Revolution and the post-revolutionary events that witnessed the consolidation of power by a hierarchical, centralized vanguard party – is a Marxist strategy *sui generis* that, whatever its fate in the years since, represented a continuity far more compelling than Lenin's different verbal pronouncements at particular moments.

3. 'Insegnamenti', *L'Ordine Nuovo* (5 May 1922), in *Scritti Politici*, pp.530–531, contains the first really strong advocacy of this position. Gramsci stressed here that, to the extent the fascist enemy was highly-disciplined and centralized, communists would have to adopt similar forms of organization to avoid being crushed.

4. Gramsci makes this point, for example, in 'Capo', *L'Ordine Nuovo* (1 March 1924), in *Scritti Politici*, pp.541–542, and in 'La Crisi italiana', *L'Ordine Nuovo* (1 September 1924), *ibid.*, pp.576–580.

5. 'L'Organizzazione base del Partito', *L'Unità* (15 August 1925), in *Scritti Politici*, pp.642–644. Whether this 'Bolshevization' of the PCI actually was designed to *replace* the councils with the cellular network was never made clear by Gramsci, but his general theoretical orientation indicates that this was extremely unlikely.

6. 'Necessità di una preparazione ideologica di massa', *Lo Stato operaio* (March–April 1931; written in May 1925), in *Scritti Politici*, pp. 600–601. Gramsci saw in the political struggle three principal subphases: the struggle to contain bourgeois power within parliamentary institutions, with its goal the creating of a new equilibrium among classes and greater freedom of organization for the working class; the struggle for the conquest of power and the construction of a new socialist state; and the struggle to build a 'dictatorship of the proletariat' capable of eliminating the technical and social obstacles that stand in the way of realizing communism.

7. 'The Study of Philosophy', *Prison Notebooks*, p.360.

8. 'State and Civil Society', *Prison Notebooks*, p.247.

9. 'The Modern Prince', *Prison Notebooks*, p.166.

10. 'State and Civil Society', *Prison Notebooks*, pp.250–251.

11. *ibid.*, pp.248–249. For an excellent discussion of this dimension of Machiavelli's thought, see Sheldon Wolin, *op. cit.*, ch. 6.

12. 'The Modern Prince', *Prison Notebooks*, p.172.
13. 'State and Civil Society', *Prison Notebooks*, p.252.
14. 'The Modern Prince', *Prison Notebooks*, p.125.
15. *ibid.*, p.134.
16. See in particular 'The Modern Prince', *Prison Notebooks*, pp.130–133. Gramsci introduced the term 'Cadornism' (after the Italian general Luigi Cadorna) to refer to the short-sighted attempts of authoritarian leaders to establish political power without winning over the support of the people they seek to lead. It was precisely this almost total failure to deal with the imperatives of consent that Gramsci found most destructive in Bordiga's early influence within the PCI.
17. 'The Modern Prince', *Prison Notebooks*, p.160.
18. *ibid.*, pp.157–158.
19. 'Notes on Italian History', *Prison Notebooks*, pp.78–80.
20. 'The Modern Prince', *Prison Notebooks*, p.132.
21. 'State and Civil Society', *Prison Notebooks*, p.240.
22. *ibid.*, p.241.
23. *ibid.*
24. *ibid.*, pp.252–253. Or: 'the protagonist of the new Prince could not in the modern epoch be an individual hero, but only the political party.' 'The Modern Prince', *Prison Notebooks*, p.147.
25. 'The Modern Prince', *Prison Notebooks*, p.151.
26. It is interesting to note that, even within the 'conjunctural' or 'war of movement' dimension of revolutionary struggle, Gramsci further identifies three 'relations of forces' that must be strategically taken into account – the social, political, and military – each with its own dynamic, yet comprehended as part of the whole process. See 'The Modern Prince', *Prison Notebooks*, pp.180–182.
27. *ibid.*, pp.204–205. What Gramsci had in mind here is something more extreme than Lenin's own position, perhaps more akin to a Blanquist kind of adventurism, but the basic argument still holds.

Epilogue / pp.119–126

1. This theme is developed in Klare, *op. cit.*
2. Franz Schurmann, 'System, Contradictions, and Revolution in America', in Roderick Aya and Norman Miller, *The New American Revolution* (Glencoe, Illinois: The Free Press 1971), pp.75–76.
3. See Herbert Gintis, 'Activism and Counter-culture: The Dialectics of

Consciousness in the Corporate State', *Telos* (Summer 1972), pp.52–53. Needless to say, the 'dialectics of consciousness' that Gintis refers to here is not something independent of structural transformation — a point that also applies to the general line of argument in this chapter.

4. Paulo Freire, *The Pedagogy of the Oppressed* (New York: Seabury Press 1971), pp.36–47.

5. *ibid.*, p.86. See also Gintis *op. cit.*, on the importance of creating a *political* counterculture by means of re-creating everyday life.

Index

abstentionism 19,80,105
Americanism and Fordism 46,131n
anarchism 11
Arato, Andrew 68,133n

Bernstein, Eduard 11
Blanquism 66,101,103,140n
'bloc' 80–81,84,109,112,117,136–37n
Bolsheviks 24,25,26,86,90,103–104, 118,139n
Bonapartism 86
Bordiga, Amadeo 14,18,61,80,82,95, 105,112–13,115,140n
bureaucracy 44–46,88,98,100
bureaucratic centralism 116,118; *see also* centralism
Bukharin, Nikolai 23,26,65,128n,133

Cadornism 140n
cadres 108
Cammett, John 130n,132n
Capital 25,26,128n
Catholicism 33,35,42–43,49,71,111, 134n
cells 104
centralism 105; *see also* bureaucratic centralism
civil society 38–39,48,53,81,113, 116–17,120,130n
'collective intellectual' 115
Colletti, Lucio 136n
Comintern 11,14,58,80,82,98,112,120
Comitati di base 98
Commissione interne 90,94
'commonsense' 29,33,39,65,70–72, 110,134n
'conjunctural' 114–16

consciousness 17–18,31,37,40,55f,78, 81,83,93,97,109,123
Council Communists 19,58,98
'counter-hegemony' 40–41,54,81,114
'crisis of authority' 130n
Critical Theory 18,20,129n; *see also* Frankfurt School
Croce, Benedetto 13,21,23,29,33,34, 35,38,42,108,111,129n, 130–131n,136n

Davidson, Alastair 131n
deradicalization 93
dialectic 23,24,33
dictatorship of the proletariat 102,139n
Direzione 52
'dual perspective' 114,116
'dual power' 13,86,97,98

economism 11,102,103,106,110
Engels, Frederick 11,23,55
Enlightenment, the 52
'ensemble of relations' 18,75,116, 120–121
'ethico-political' 34,38,108,116
'external element' 70,72,99

factory councils 13,85f,103
family 44–45
Fascism 46,47,57,72,82,103–104,113
Feuerbach, Ludwig 23
Fiat 90,95
Fiori, Giuseppe 15,127n
Fordism 44
Frankfurt School 12,18,129n
Freire, Paulo 123,141n
French Revolution 24–25,49,111
Futurism 60

General Confederation of Labour (CGIL) 88–89,91
Genovese, Eugene 130n
Gentile, Giovanni 31
German Social Democracy 24,46
Germany 48–49,56
Gintis, Herbert 140n,141n
Gramsci, Antonio, stages of his thought 12–15; *see also* particular subjects
Graziadei, Antonio 29
Il Grido del Popolo 127n,132n,134n

Hartz, Louis 131–32n
Hegel, G.W.F. 23,34,38
hegemony 17,34,36f,71–72,83,87,92, 96,97,99,108,110,113,114,115,121, 122
historicism 29
Hoare, Quintin 127n
Hobsbawm, Eric 133n,135n
Horkheimer, Max 129n
Hughes, H. Stuart 130n

idealism 22,37
ideological-cultural struggle 17–18,60, 120
'integrated culture' 17,41,74,99,123
intellectuals 33,74,75–79,125,135n; 'organic' 77–79
internationalism 112–13
Italian capitalism 109
Italian city-states 106–107
Italian Communist Party (PCI) 14,15, 29,38,61,80,82,97,98,103,105,109, 111,112,113,120,139n
Italian Socialist Party (PSI) 12–13,22, 24,29,58,59–60,82,89,91,94,96,112

Jacobinism 18,69,78,83,93,96,100,101, 106,108–11,116
Jay, Martin 129n

Kautsky, Karl 11,23,78
Kolakowski, Leszek 12
Korsch, Karl 12,16,21,28,58,128n, 129n

Labriola, Antonio 21,22,58
Lawner, Lynne 127n,129n,132n,138n
Lenin, V.I. 12,16,19,21,38,55,65, 68–69,70,74,79,83,102–103,104, 108,114,115,130n,133n,138–39n
Lukacs, Georg 12,21,40,57,58,65, 67–68,74,86,133n,134n
Luxemburg, Rosa 11,58,63,65–67,68, 74,79,133n,134n
Lyons Party Congress 61,80,112
Lyons Theses 38,82,95

Machiavelli, Niccolo 106–11,114
Magri, Lucio 133n,136n
Il Manifesto 136n
Mao Tse-tung 130n
Marcuse, Herbert 12,18,46,129n
Marinetti, Filippo 60
Marx, Karl 11,23,25,28,37,45,47,55, 101–102,128n
Marxism, Hegelian 21,29,32,58,63,78, 134n; mechanistic 22–23,68,70; orthodox 21–22,63,83,106,116
Marzani, Carlo 129n
materialism 22–23
Mezzogiorno 73,82,111,112,136n
Michels, Robert 45–46
'modern prince' 115
Montesquieu, C. 38
Moore, Stanley 103,138n
'myth prince' 114

nationalism 111,113
national-popular movement 19,49,82, 83,108,112,114,136n
New Left 119
Nowell-Smith, Geoffrey 127n

L'Ordine Nuovo 13,14,15,26,60–61, 74,85f,103,127n,132n,137–38n
'organic' 52,114–15,117
'organic centralism' 118

parliamentarism 104
'passive revolution' 50
Pirandello, Luigi 25

Plekhanov, George 11,23,26
politics 101–112
politics, primacy of 102,105,109, 112,114–16
Popular Front 80,82,119
positivism 25,26,27,102
pragmatism 124–25
praxis 17,27,30,35,53,124
prediction 30
'prefigurative struggle' 13,90,93–94, 95,98,100,137n
Prince 108
Protestantism 43–44

Quaderni del Carcere 14,15,21,26,27, 31,32,35,36,38,40,61–63,70,71,74,80, 81,95,96,105,107,114,115,118,119, 120,127n,128n,129n,130n,131n, 132n,133n,134n,135n,136n

rationalization 45–47
Reformation, the 43,49,52,79
reformism 39,59,73,88–89,110
Reich, Wilhelm 19,44,56–58,132n
'reification' 68
religion 29,33,34
Renaissance 49
Resistance, the 98,113–14
revolutionary party 18,86,95,97,99, 101f
La rivoluzione contro il 'Capitale' 26, 127n
Il Risorgimento 19,50,111
Russia 25,48,53,66,103,113

Salinari, Carlo 127n,130n
Salvemini, Gaetano 109
Sartre, Jean-Paul 12
Schurmann, Franz 122,140n
Schucht, Tatiana 17
scientism 59
Scritti Politici 127n,132n,134n, 137–38n,139n
Second International 11,13,16,21,24, 39,54,55,58,79,83,90,101,113
Second Risorgimento 112

sectarianism 61
sexual relations 44–45
'Socialism in One Country' 113
Social Democracy 61,93
Sorel, Georges 35,63,79,108,132–33
Soviets 90,94,118
Soviet Union 113,118
Spinella, Mario 127n,130n
spontaneism 65,68,70,74–75,83, 100,102,109
Spriano, Paolo 127n
Stalin, J. 19,113,119
state, the 73,116
Lo Stato operaio 14,127n,139n
Stedman-Jones, Gareth 134n
subjectivism 35,65
superstructure 36,38,101–102,106,116
Syndicalism 110,132n

Tasca, Angelo 90
Taylorism 46,47
technology 44–45,47
Terracini, Umberto 90
theorist, role of 27,32,33,124–26
Togliatti, Palmiro 90
totality 78,115,122
trade unions 86–89,94
Trasformismo 50
Trotsky, Leon 53
Turin Socialists 89–91,97,137n
'two revolutions' 91–92

L'Unità 127n,132n
united front 61,80,82,136n
United States 44–45,47,50–52, 131–32

'voluntarism' 31,35,105,117
'volunteer action' 116

'war of manœuvre' 114
'war of position' 53,86,115,131n
Weber, Max 38,43,45,56
Williams, Gwyn 130n
Wolin, Sheldon 138n,139n
women 44–45
workers' control 88,92–93,95

Alex Callinicos

Althusser's Marxism

Alex Callinicos places Althusser's work in the context of the two main traditions of marxist philosophy, Engels and the orthodox 'dialectical materialism' of the Second International, Lukacs and the Hegelian marxism of the 1920s. He provides an introduction to the entire range of Althusser's ideas and traces, for the first time in English, their development and transformation. The result is an attempt to judge Althusser, not simply as a philosopher, but as a marxist.

Available from
Pluto Press
Unit 10 Spencer Court, 7 Chalcot Road,
London NW1 8LH

Complete list of
Pluto books and pamphlets
available on request

Martin Shaw

Marxism and Social Science
the roots of social knowledge

Martin Shaw argues that the crisis of the social sciences is not simply one of intellectual direction. It grows from the social sciences' roots in the industrial, educational and ideological systems of capitalist society discussed in this book. The solutions are not just theoretical – theory must be related to practice, within academic institutions as well as in the wider class struggle.

A companion volume to *Marxism versus Sociology: a guide to reading*, also by Martin Shaw.

Available from
Pluto Press
Unit 10 Spencer Court, 7 Chalcot Road,
London NW1 8LH

Complete list of
Pluto books and pamphlets
available on request